American History
Beginnings Through Reconstruction

Jonathan D. Kantrowitz, Editor

Class Pack ISBN: 978-0-7827-1275-9 • Student Book ISBN: 978-0-7827-1274-2
Copyright © 2004 Queue, Inc.

Queue, Inc. • 80 Hathaway Drive, Stratford, CT 06615
(800) 232-2224 • Fax: (800) 775-2729 • www.qworkbooks.com

Table of Contents

CHAPTER 1
Early America—Beginnings to 1585

THE FIRST AMERICANS

At the height of the Ice Age, between 34,000 and 30,000 B.C., much of the world's water was contained in vast continental ice sheets. As a result, the Bering Sea was hundreds of meters below its current level. A land bridge, known as Beringia, emerged between Asia and North America. At its peak, Beringia is thought to have been some one thousand five hundred kilometers wide. A moist and treeless tundra, it was covered with grasses and plant life. It attracted large animals that early humans hunted for their survival.

The first people to reach North America almost certainly did so without knowing they had crossed into a new continent. They would have been following game, as their ancestors had for thousands of years, along the Siberian coast and then across the land bridge.

Once in Alaska, it would take these first North Americans thousands of years more to work their way through the openings in great glaciers south to what is now the United States. Evidence of early life in North America continues to be found. Little of it, however, can be reliably dated before 12,000 B.C. A recent discovery of a hunting lookout in northern Alaska, for example, may date from almost that time. So too may the finely crafted spear points and items found near Clovis, New Mexico.

Similar artifacts have been found at sites throughout North and South America, indicating that life was probably already well established in much of the Western Hemisphere by some time prior to 10,000 B.C.

Around that time, the mammoth began to die out and the bison took its place as a principal source of food and hides for these early North Americans. Over time, as more and more species of large game vanished—whether from overhunting or natural causes—plants, berries, and seeds became an increasingly important part of the early American diet. Gradually, foraging and the first attempts at primitive agriculture appeared. Indians in what is now central Mexico led the way, cultivating corn, squash, and beans, perhaps as early as 8,000 B.C. Slowly, this knowledge spread northward.

By 3,000 B.C., a primitive type of corn was being grown in the river valleys of New Mexico and Arizona. Then the first signs of irrigation began to appear, and by 300 B.C., signs of early village life.

By the first centuries A.D., the Hohokum were living in settlements near what is now Phoenix, Arizona, where they built ball courts and pyramid-like mounds reminiscent of those found in Mexico, as well as a canal and irrigation system.

1

1. The land bridge between Asia and North America

    a. appeared after the Ice Age.
    b. appeared after the continental ice sheets had melted.
    c. was known as the Bering Sea.
    d. was known as Beringia.

2. The first people to cross into North America

    a. were seeking a new home.
    b. were seeking plants and grass for their animals.
    c. were following large animals.
    d. were glad to see a bridge appear.

3. The first evidence of human life in North America may be

    a. reliably dated before 12,000 B.C.
    b. finely crafted spear points in Clovis, New Mexico.
    c. a hunting lookout in Clovis, New Mexico.
    d. finely crafted spear points in Alaska.

4. Humans probably had entered much of North and South America by

    a. 12,000 B.C.
    b. 10,000 *B.C.*
    c. 8,000 B.C.
    d. 3,000 B.C.

5. North Americans turned to foraging because

    a. the mammoth and other large animals died out.
    b. the bison died out.
    c. the Indians of central Mexico began cultivating corn, squash, and beans.
    d. they did not want to eat plants, berries, and beans.

6. Agriculture did not reach what is now the United States until

    a. 12,000 B.C.
    b. 10,000 B.C.
    c. 8,000 B.C.
    d. 3,000 *B.C.*

7. The Hohokum lifestyle appears to have been much of that of

    a. their ancestors of Asia.
    b. the first settlers in America.
    c. earlier civilizations in Mexico.
    d. later civilizations in South America.

MOUND BUILDERS AND PUEBLOS

The first Indian group to build mounds in what is now the United States are often called the Adenans. They began constructing earthen burial sites and fortifications around 600 B.C. Some mounds from that era are in the shape of birds or serpents. They probably served religious purposes not yet fully understood.

The Adenans appear to have been absorbed or displaced by various groups collectively known as Hopewellians. One of the most important centers of their culture was found in southern Ohio, where the remains of several thousand of these mounds still remain. Believed to be great traders, the Hopewellians used and exchanged tools and materials across a wide region of hundreds of kilometers.

By around 500 A.D., the Hopewellians also disappeared, gradually giving way to a broad group of tribes generally known as the Mississippians or Temple Mound culture. One city, Cahokia, just east of St. Louis, Missouri, is thought to have had a population of about twenty thousand at its peak in the early 12th century. At the center of the city stood a huge earthen mound, flatted at the top, which was thirty meters high and thirty-seven hectares at the base. Eighty other mounds have been found nearby.

Cities such as Cahokia depended on a combination of hunting, foraging, trading, and agriculture for their food and supplies. Influenced by the thriving societies to the south, they evolved into complex hierarchical societies that took slaves and practiced human sacrifice.

In what is now the southwest United States, the Anasazi, ancestors of the modern Hopi Indians, began building stone and adobe pueblos around the year 900. These unique and amazing apartment-like structures were often built along cliff faces; the most famous, the "cliff palace" of Mesa Verde, Colorado, had over two hundred rooms. Another site, the Pueblo Bonito ruins along New Mexico's Chaco River, once contained more than eight hundred rooms.

Perhaps the most affluent of the pre-Columbian American Indians lived in the Pacific northwest, where the natural abundance of fish and raw materials made food supplies plentiful and permanent villages possible as early as 1,000 B.C. The opulence of their "potlatch" gatherings remains a standard for extravagance and festivity probably unmatched in early American history.

1. Several thousand mounds in southern Ohio are all that is left of the _____ culture.

    a. Adenan
    b. Hopewellian
    c. Mississippian
    d. Temple Mound

2. The Hopewellians and the Mississippians appear to have _____ across a wide area.

    a. hunted
    b. farmed
    c. migrated
    d. traded

3. The Mississippians emerged around

   a. 600 B.C.
   b. 500 *A.D.*
   c. 100 A.D.
   d. 1100 A.D.

4. _____ had a population of 20,000.

   a. Cahokia
   b. Mesa Verde
   c. Pueblo Bunita
   d. Temple Mound

5. The Native Americans with the most abundant resources were located in

   a. the Ohio River Valley.
   b. the Missouri-Mississippi Run Valley.
   c. the southwest.
   d. the northwest.

NATIVE AMERICAN CULTURES

The America that greeted the first Europeans was, thus, far from an empty wilderness. It is now thought that as many people lived in the Western Hemisphere as in Western Europe at that time—about forty million.

Estimates of the number of Native Americans living in what is now the United States at the onset of European colonization range from two to eighteen million, with most historians tending toward the lower figure. What is certain is the devastating effect that European disease had on the indigenous population practically from the time of initial contact. Smallpox, in particular, ravaged whole communities and is thought to have been a much more direct cause of the precipitous decline in Indian population in the 1600s than the numerous wars and skirmishes with European settlers.

Indian customs and culture at the time were extraordinarily diverse, as could be expected, given the expanse of the land and the many different environments to which they had adapted. Some generalizations, however, are possible.

Most tribes, particularly in the wooded eastern region and the Midwest, combined aspects of hunting, gathering, and the cultivation of maize and other products for their food supplies. In many cases, the women were responsible for farming and the distribution of food, while the men hunted and participated in war.

By all accounts, Indian society in North America was closely tied to the land. Identification with nature and the elements was integral to religious beliefs. Indian life was essentially clan-oriented and communal, with children allowed more freedom and tolerance than was the European custom of the day.

4

Although some North American tribes developed a type of hieroglyphic to preserve certain texts, Indian culture was primarily oral, with a high value placed on the recounting of tales and dreams. Clearly, there was a good deal of trade among various groups and strong evidence exists that neighboring tribes maintained extensive and formal relations—both friendly and hostile.

1. Most historians believe that _____ million people lived in the Western Hemisphere before European discovery.
   a. two
   b. eighteen
   c. forty
   d. eighty

2. Most historians believe that _____ million people lived in what is now the United States before European discovery.
   a. two
   b. eighteen
   c. forty
   d. eighty

3. Indian tribes suffered the most casualties from
   a. starvation.
   b. disease.
   c. attacks by Europeans.
   d. attacks by other Indians.

4. Europeans on the whole were much _____ than the Indian society of that time.
   a. closer to nature
   b. more likely to hunt for food
   c. more clan-oriented and communal
   d. stricter with their children

5. The Indian tribe in general were
   a. isolated.
   b. literate.
   c. oriented to storytelling.
   d. invariably hostile to one another.

MORE ABOUT THE ANASAZI

Time-worn pueblos and dramatic "cliff towns," set amid the stark, rugged mesas and canyons of Colorado and New Mexico, mark the settlements of some of the earliest inhabitants of North America, the Anasazi (a Navajo word meaning "ancient ones").

By 500 A.D., the Anasazi had established some of the first identifiable villages in the American Southwest, where they hunted and grew crops of corn, squash, and beans. The Anasazi flourished over the centuries, developing sophisticated dams and irrigation systems; creating a masterful, distinctive pottery tradition; and carving intricate, multi-room dwellings into the sheer sides of cliffs that remain among the most striking archaeological sites in the United States today.

Yet by the year 1300, they had abandoned their settlements, leaving their pottery, implements, even clothing—as though they intended to return—and seemingly disappeared into history. Their homeland remained empty of human beings for more than a century—until the arrival of new tribes, such as the Navajo and the Ute, followed by the Spanish and other European settlers.

The story of the Anasazi is tied inextricably to the beautiful but harsh environment in which they chose to live. Early settlements, consisting of simple pithouses scooped out of the ground, evolved into sunken kivas that served as meeting and religious sites. Later generations developed the masonry techniques for building square, stone pueblos. However, the most dramatic change in Anasazi living—for reasons that are still unclear—was the move to the cliff sides below the flat-topped mesas, where the Anasazi carved their amazing, multilevel dwellings.

The Anasazi lived in a communal society that evolved very slowly over the centuries. They traded with other peoples in the region, but signs of warfare are few and isolated. And although the Anasazi certainly had religious and other leaders, as well as skilled artisans, social or class distinctions were virtually nonexistent.

Religious and social motives undoubtedly played a part in the building of the cliff communities and their final abandonment. But the struggle to raise food in an increasingly difficult environment was probably the paramount factor. As populations grew, farmers planted larger areas on the mesas, causing some communities to farm marginal lands, while others left the mesa tops for the cliffs. However, the Anasazi couldn't halt the steady loss of the land's fertility from constant use, nor withstand the region's cyclical droughts. Analysis of tree rings, for example, shows that a final drought lasting twenty-three years, from 1276 to 1299, finally forced the last groups of Anasazi to leave permanently.

Although the Anasazi dispersed from their ancestral homeland, they did not disappear. Their legacy remains in the remarkable archaeological record that they left behind, and in the Hopi, Zuni, and other Pueblo peoples who are their descendants.

1. The final developments in Anasazi housing were

   a. pithouses scooped out of the ground.
   b. sunken kivas.
   c. square, stone pueblos.
   d. multi-level, cliff-side dwellings.

2. The Anasazi's accomplishments did **not** include

   a. conquest of the Navajos and the Utes.
   b. beautiful pottery.
   c. dams and irrigation.
   d. intricate multi-room dwellings.

3. The Anasazi probably abandoned their homes because

   a. they had never learned farming.
   b. they were conquered by the Spanish.
   c. the buffalo herds disappeared.
   d. a prolonged drought deprived them of crops.

THE FIRST EUROPEANS

The first Europeans to arrive in North America—at least the first for whom there is solid evidence—were Norse, traveling west from Greenland, where Erik the Red had founded a settlement around the year 985. In 1001, his son Leif is thought to have explored the northeast coast of what is now Canada and spent at least one winter there.

While Norse sagas suggest that Viking sailors explored the Atlantic coast of North America down as far as the Bahamas, such claims remain unproven. In 1963, however, the ruins of some Norse houses dating from that era were discovered at L'Anse-aux-Meadows in northern Newfoundland, thus supporting at least some of the claims the Norse sagas make.

In 1497, just five years after Christopher Columbus landed in the Caribbean looking for a western route to Asia, a Venetian sailor named John Cabot arrived in Newfoundland on a mission for the British king. Although fairly quickly forgotten, Cabot's journey was later to provide the basis for British claims to North America. It also opened the way to the rich fishing grounds off George's Banks, to which European fishermen, particularly the Portuguese, were soon making regular visits.

Columbus, of course, never saw the mainland United States, but the first explorations of the continental United States were launched from the Spanish possessions that he helped establish. The first of these took place in 1513 when a group of men under Juan Ponce de Leon landed on the Florida coast near the present city of St. Augustine.

With the conquest of Mexico in 1522, the Spanish further solidified their position in the Western Hemisphere. The ensuing discoveries added to Europe's knowledge of what was now named America—after the Italian Amerigo Vespucci, who wrote a widely popular account of his voyages to a "New World." By 1529, reliable maps of the Atlantic coastline from Labrador to Tierra del Fuego had been drawn up, although it would take more than another century before hope of discovering a "Northwest Passage" to Asia would be completely abandoned.

Among the most significant early Spanish explorations was that of Hernando De Soto, a veteran conquistador who had accompanied Francisco Pizarro during the conquest of Peru. Leaving Havana in 1539, De Soto's expedition landed in Florida and ranged through the southeastern United States as far as the Mississippi River in search of riches.

Another Spaniard, Francisco Coronado, set out from Mexico in 1540 in search of the mythical Seven Cities of Cibola. Coronado's travels took him to the Grand Canyon and Kansas, but failed to reveal the gold or treasure his men sought.

However, Coronado's party did leave the peoples of the region a remarkable, if unintended gift: enough horses escaped from his party to transform life on the Great Plains. Within a few generations, the Plains Indians had become masters of horsemanship, greatly expanding the range and scope of their activities.

While the Spanish were pushing up from the south, the northern portion of the present-day United States was slowly being revealed through the journeys of men such as Giovanni da Verrazano. A Florentine who sailed for the French, Verrazano made landfall in North Carolina in 1524, then sailed north along the Atlantic coast past what is now New York harbor.

A decade later, the Frenchman Jacques Cartier set sail with the hope—like the other Europeans before him—of finding a sea passage to Asia. Cartier's expeditions along the St. Lawrence River laid the foundations for the French claims to North America, which were to last until 1763.

Following the collapse of their first Quebec colony in the 1540s, French Huguenots attempted to settle the northern coast of Florida two decades later. The Spanish, viewing the French as a threat to their trade route along the Gulf Stream, destroyed the colony in 1565. Ironically, the leader of the Spanish forces, Pedro Menendez, would soon establish a town not far away—St. Augustine. It was the first permanent European settlement in what would become the United States.

The great wealth that poured into Spain from the colonies in Mexico, the Caribbean, and Peru provoked great interest on the part of the other European powers. With time, emerging maritime nations such as England, drawn in part by Francis Drake's successful raids on Spanish treasure ships, began to take interest in the New World.

In 1578, Humphrey Gilbert, the author of a treatise on the search for the Northwest Passage, received a patent from Queen Elizabeth to colonize the "heathen and barbarous landes" in the New World which other European nations had not yet claimed. It would be five years before his efforts could begin. When he was lost at sea, his half-brother Walter Raleigh took up the mission.

In 1585, Raleigh established the first British colony in North America, on Roanoke Island off the coast of North Carolina. It was later abandoned, and a second effort two years later also proved a failure. It would be twenty years before the British would try again. This time—at Jamestown in 1607—the colony would succeed, and North America would enter a new era.

1. There is strong evidence of the Viking discovery of America in

    a. Iceland.
    b. Greenland.
    c. Newfoundland.
    d. the Bahamas.

2. The first European to explore the North American coast was probably

    a. Erik the Red.
    b. Leif Ericsson.
    c. Christopher Columbus.
    d. Juan Ponce de Leon.

3. The first exploration of what is now the United States was under the direction of

    a. John Cabot.
    b. Amerigo Vespucci.
    c. Christopher Columbus.
    d. Juan Ponce de Leon.

4. Christopher Columbus, John Cabot, Amerigo Vespucci, and Giovanni da Verrazona all

    a. were Italian.
    b. were sailors from Spain.
    c. had a country named after them.
    d. had two continents named after them.

8

5. The southeastern U.S. was extensively explored by

    a. Amerigo Vespucci.
    b. Francisco Pizarro.
    c. Hernando De Soto.
    d. Francisco Coronado.

6. The Plains Indians owed their primary means of transportation to

    a. Amerigo Vespucci.
    b. Francisco Pizarro.
    c. Hernando De Soto.
    d. Francisco Coronado.

7. The British claims to North America were based on the voyages of

    a. Portuguese fisherman.
    b. John Cabot.
    c. Jacques Cartier.
    d. Francis Drake.

8. The first permanent European settlement in North America was founded by

    a. French Huguenots.
    b. Pedro Menendez.
    c. Humphrey Gilbert.
    d. Walter Raleigh.

9. The Viking discovery of North America was in

    a. 985.
    b. 1001.
    c. 1492.
    d. 1963.

10. John Cabot arrived in Newfoundland _____ years after Leif Ericsson.

    a. 496
    b. 1492
    c. 1497
    d. 1963

11. Ponce de Leon landed in Florida in

    a. 1513.
    b. 1522.
    c. 1529.
    d. 1539.

12. Hernando De Soto landed in Florida in

    a. 1513.
    b. 1522.
    c. 1529.
    d. 1539.

13. The Spanish destroyed the French colony in Florida in

    a. 1524.
    b. 1534.
    c. 1560.
    d. 1565.

14. The first British colony in North America was established in

    a. Virginia.
    b. North Carolina.
    c. Massachusetts.
    d. New York.

15. The first British colony in North America was established in

    a. 1578.
    b. 1585.
    c. 1607.
    d. 1620.

Chapter 1
Questions for Further Research

1. Explain the origins of the first Americans and contrast them with Native Americans' own beliefs concerning their origins in the Americas.

2. Trace the spread of human societies and the rise of diverse cultures from hunter-gatherers to urban dwellers in the Americas.

3. Compare food sources, shelter, and cultural patterns of Native American societies such as the Iroquois and Pueblo or Northwest and Southeast Indian societies.

4. Compare the different ideas that Native Americans and Europeans held about how the land should be used.

5. Were Native American societies "primitive," as the first Europeans to encounter them believed?

6. Compare Native American and European outlooks and values on the eve of "the great convergence."

7. How did geographical, scientific, and technological factors contribute to the age of exploration?

8. Describe the stages of European oceanic and overland exploration from 1492 to 1700.

9. Evaluate the significance of Columbus's voyages and his interactions with indigenous peoples.

10. Explain how religious influences and rivalries affected colonization in the Americas.

11. Describe the social composition of the early Spanish settlers and compare their motives for exploration and colonization.

12. What kind of architecture, skills, labor systems, and agriculture did the Spanish explorers find?

CHAPTER 2
Colonization and Settlement (1585–1700)

EARLY SETTLEMENTS

The early 1600s saw the beginning of a great tide of emigration from Europe to North America. Spanning more than three centuries, this movement grew from a trickle of a few hundred English colonists to a flood of millions of newcomers. Impelled by powerful and diverse motivations, they built a new civilization on the northern part of the continent.

The first English immigrants to what is now the United States crossed the Atlantic long after thriving Spanish colonies had been established in Mexico, the West Indies, and South America. Like all early travelers to the New World, they came in small, overcrowded ships. During their six- to twelve-week voyages, they lived on meager rations. Many died of disease; ships were often battered by storms and some were lost at sea.

Most European emigrants left their homelands to escape political oppression, to seek the freedom to practice their religion, or for adventure and opportunities denied them at home. Between 1620 and 1635, economic difficulties swept England. Many people could not find work. Even skilled artisans could earn little more than a bare living. Poor crop yields added to the distress. In addition, the Industrial Revolution had created a burgeoning textile industry, which demanded an ever-increasing supply of wool to keep the looms running. Landlords enclosed farmlands and evicted the peasants in favor of sheep cultivation. Colonial expansion became an outlet for this displaced peasant population.

The colonists' first glimpse of the new land was a vista of dense woods. The settlers might not have survived had it not been for the help of friendly Indians, who taught them how to grow native plants—pumpkin, squash, beans, and corn. In addition, the vast, virgin forests, extending nearly 2,100 kilometers along the eastern seaboard, proved a rich source of game and firewood. They also provided abundant raw materials used to build houses, furniture, ships, and profitable cargoes for export.

Although the new continent was remarkably endowed by nature, trade with Europe was vital for articles the settlers could not produce. The coast served the immigrants well. The whole length of shore provided innumerable inlets and harbors. Only two areas—North Carolina and southern New Jersey—lacked harbors for ocean-going vessels.

Majestic rivers—the Kennebec, Hudson, Delaware, Susquehanna, Potomac, and numerous others—linked lands between the coast and the Appalachian Mountains with the sea. Only one river, however, the St. Lawrence—dominated by the French in Canada—offered a water passage to the Great Lakes and into the heart of the continent. Dense forests, the resistance of some Indian tribes, and the formidable barrier of the Appalachian Mountains discouraged settlement beyond the coastal plain. Only trappers and traders ventured into the wilderness. For the first hundred years, the colonists built their settlements compactly along the coast.

Political considerations influenced many people's decision to move to America. In the 1630s, arbitrary rule by England's Charles I gave impetus to the migration to the New World. The subsequent revolt and triumph of Charles's opponents under Oliver Cromwell in the 1640s led many cavaliers—"king's men"—to cast their lot in Virginia. In the German-speaking regions of Europe, the oppressive policies of various petty princes—particularly with regard to religion—and the devastation caused by a long series of wars helped swell the movement to America in the late 17th and 18th centuries.

The coming of colonists in the 17th century entailed careful planning and management, as well as considerable expense and risk. Settlers had to be transported nearly five thousand kilometers across the sea. They needed utensils, clothing, seed, tools, building materials, livestock, arms, and ammunition.

In contrast to the colonization policies of other countries and other periods, the emigration from England was not directly sponsored by the government, but by private groups of individuals whose chief motive was profit.

1. The latest settlements were

    a. Spanish colonies in Mexico.
    b. Spanish colonies in South America.
    c. Spanish colonies in West Indies.
    d. English colonies in North America.

2. The first impetus of English emigrants to settle in America was **not** related to

    a. economic difficulties.
    b. the individual Revolution.
    c. war with France.
    d. sheep cultivation.

3. The first colonists needed Indian help

    a. to grow crops.
    b. to hunt game.
    c. to cut firewood.
    d. to build with wood.

4. North Carolina and New Jersey were the only areas that lacked

    a. vast, virgin forests.
    b. raw materials for trade.
    c. profitable cargoes for export.
    d. harbors.

5. Settlement was limited to the coast by all of the following **except**

    a. rivers.
    b. mountains.
    c. forests.
    d. hostile Indians.

6. In German-speaking areas, migration was hastened by

    a. King Charles I's oppression.
    b. King Charles I's overthrow.
    c. Oliver Cromwell.
    d. wars and religious intolerance.

12

JAMESTOWN

The first of the British colonies to take hold in North America was Jamestown. On the basis of a charter that King James I granted to the Virginia (or London) Company, a group of about one hundred men set out for the Chesapeake Bay in 1607. Seeking to avoid conflict with the Spanish, they chose a site about sixty kilometers up the James River from the bay.

Made up of townsmen and adventurers more interested in finding gold than farming, the group was unequipped by temperament or ability to embark upon a completely new life in the wilderness. Among them, Captain John Smith emerged as the dominant figure. Despite quarrels, starvation, and Indian attacks, his ability to enforce discipline held the little colony together through its first year.

In 1609, Smith returned to England and, in his absence, the colony descended into anarchy. During the winter of 1609–1610, the majority of the colonists succumbed to disease. Only sixty of the original three hundred settlers were still alive by May 1610. That same year, the town of Henrico (now Richmond) was established farther up the James River.

It was not long, however, before a development occurred that revolutionized Virginia's economy. In 1612, John Rolfe began cross-breeding imported tobacco seed from the West Indies with native plants and produced a new variety that was pleasing to European taste. The first shipment of this tobacco reached London in 1614. Within a decade, it had become Virginia's chief source of revenue.

Prosperity did not come quickly, however, and the death rate from disease and Indian attacks remained extraordinarily high. Between 1607 and 1624, approximately fourteen thousand people migrated to the colony, yet only 1,132 were living there in 1624. On recommendation of a royal commission, the king dissolved the Virginia Company and made it a royal colony that year.

1. Jamestown only survived because of

   a. quarrels.
   b. starvation.
   c. Indian attacks.
   d. John Smith's leadership.

2. By 1610, _____ settlers had come to Jamestown.

   a. 60
   b. 100
   c. 300
   d. 14,000

3. By 1624, how many settlers remained in Virginia?

   a. 60
   b. 300
   c. 1,132
   d. 14,000

4. Virginia's problems would have been even worse if not for John Rolfe's work to develop

   a.tobacco.
   b. cotton fields.
   c. gold mines.
   d. lumberyards.

5. The Virginia Company was dissolved in

   a. 1607.
   b. 1610.
   c. 1641.
   d. 1624.

MASSACHUSETTS

During the religious upheavals of the 16th century, a body of men and women called Puritans sought to reform the Established Church of England from within. Essentially, they demanded that the rituals and structures associated with Roman Catholicism be replaced by simpler Protestant forms of faith and worship. Their reformist ideas, by destroying the unity of the state church, threatened to divide the people and to undermine royal authority.

In 1607, a small group of Separatists—a radical sect of Puritans who did not believe the Established Church could ever be reformed—departed for Leyden, Holland, where the Dutch granted them asylum. However, the Calvinist Dutch restricted them mainly to low-paid laboring jobs. Some members of the congregation grew dissatisfied with this discrimination and resolved to emigrate to the New World.

In 1620, a group of Leyden Puritans secured a land patent from the Virginia Company, and a group of one hundred and one men, women, and children set out for Virginia on board the *Mayflower*. A storm sent them far north and they landed in New England on Cape Cod. Believing themselves outside the jurisdiction of any organized government, the men drafted a formal agreement to abide by "just and equal laws" drafted by leaders of their own choosing. This was the Mayflower Compact.

In December, the *Mayflower* reached Plymouth harbor; the Pilgrims began to build their settlement during the winter. Nearly half the colonists died of exposure and disease, but neighboring Wampanoag Indians provided information that would sustain them: how to grow maize. By the next fall, the Pilgrims had a plentiful crop of corn, and a growing trade based on furs and lumber.

A new wave of immigrants arrived on the shores of Massachusetts Bay in 1630, bearing a grant from King Charles I to establish a colony. Many of them were Puritans whose religious practices were increasingly prohibited in England. Their leader John Winthrop openly set out to create a

14

"city upon a hill" in the New World. By this he meant a place where Puritans would live in strict accordance with their religious beliefs.

The Massachusetts Bay Colony was to play a significant role in the development of the entire New England region, in part because Winthrop and his Puritan colleagues were able to bring their charter with them. Thus the authority for the colony's government resided in Massachusetts, not in England.

Under the charter's provisions, power rested with the General Court, which was made up of "freemen" required to be members of the Puritan Church. This guaranteed that the Puritans would be the dominant political as well as religious force in the colony. It was the General Court that elected the governor. For most of the next generation, this would be John Winthrop.

The rigid orthodoxy of the Puritan rule was not to everyone's liking. One of the first to challenge the General Court openly was a young clergyman named Roger Williams, who objected to the colony's seizure of Indian lands and its relations with the Church of England.

Banished from Massachusetts Bay, he purchased land from the Narragansett Indians in what is now Providence, Rhode Island, in 1636. There he set up the first American colony where complete separation of church and state as well as freedom of religion was practiced.

So-called heretics like Williams were not the only ones who left Massachusetts. Orthodox Puritans, seeking better lands and opportunities, soon began leaving Massachusetts Bay Colony. News of the fertility of the Connecticut River Valley, for instance, attracted the interest of farmers having a difficult time with poor land. By the early 1630s, many were ready to brave the danger of Indian attacks to obtain level ground and deep, rich soil. These new communities often eliminated church membership as a prerequisite for voting, thereby extending the franchise to ever larger numbers of men.

At the same time, other settlements began cropping up along the New Hampshire and Maine coasts, as more and more immigrants sought the land and liberty the New World seemed to offer.

1. Separatists were

    a. Roman Catholic.
    b. Puritans who believed the Established Church of England could be reformed.
    c. Puritans who believed the Established Church of England could not be reformed.
    d. Calvinist Dutch.

2. The _____ granted the Leyden Puritans a land patent.

    a. Virginia Colony
    b. Virginia Company
    c. Separatists
    d. Calvinist Dutch

3. The _____ discriminated against the Puritans.

    a. Virginia Colony
    b. Virginia Company
    c. Separatists
    d. Calvinist Dutch

4. The *Mayflower* set sail for

   a. Virginia.
   b. Cape Cod.
   c. Plymouth.
   d. Boston.

5. The Mayflower Compact was signed because

   a. the storm had scared people.
   b. Massachusetts was colder than Virginia.
   c. there was no organized government in Massachusetts.
   d. the Wampanoag Indians required it in order to provide assistance.

6. More immigrants came to Massachusetts

   a. before 1630.
   b. before King Charles I provided a grant.
   c. before John Winthrop.
   d. after persecution of Puritans increased in England.

7. The General Court of Massachusetts

   a. consisted of many different religions.
   b. had little influence.
   c. elected John Winthrop governor for a long time.
   d. elected Roger Williams governor for a long time.

8. Rhode Island was the first colony

   a. established outside Massachusetts.
   b. to practice religious toleration.
   c. to seize land from the Indians.
   d. to live in strict accordance with religious beliefs.

9. Massachusetts Bay Colony residents seeking economic opportunity and greater freedoms soon spread to all of the following **except**

   a. the Connecticut River Valley of Massachusetts and Connecticut.
   b. New Hampshire.
   c. Maine.
   d. New York.

NEW NETHERLAND AND MARYLAND

Hired by the Dutch East India Company, Henry Hudson in 1609 explored the area around what is now New York City and the river that bears his name. He sailed to a point probably north of Albany, New York. Subsequent Dutch voyages laid the basis for their claims and early settlements in the area.

Like the French to the north, the first interest of the Dutch was the fur trade. To this end, the Dutch cultivated close relations with the Five Nations of the Iroquois. They were the key to the heartland from which the furs came. In 1617, Dutch settlers built a fort at the junction of the Hudson and the Mohawk Rivers, where Albany now stands.

Settlement on the island of Manhattan began in the early 1620s. In 1624, the island was purchased from local Indians for the reported price of $24. It was promptly renamed New Amsterdam.

In order to attract settlers to the Hudson River region, the Dutch encouraged a type of feudal aristocracy, known as the "patroon" system. The first of these huge estates were established in 1630 along the Hudson River.

Under the patroon system, any stockholder, or patroon, who could bring fifty adults to his estate over a four-year period was given a twenty-five-kilometer riverfront plot, exclusive fishing and hunting privileges, and civil and criminal jurisdiction over his lands. In turn, he provided livestock, tools, and buildings. The tenants paid the patroon rent and gave him first option on surplus crops.

Further to the south, a Swedish trading company with ties to the Dutch attempted to set up its first settlement along the Delaware River three years later. Without the resources to consolidate its position, New Sweden was gradually absorbed into New Netherland, and later, Pennsylvania and Delaware.

In 1632, the Calvert family obtained a charter for land north of the Potomac River from King Charles I in what became known as Maryland. As the charter did not expressly prohibit the establishment of non-Protestant churches, the family encouraged fellow Catholics to settle there. Maryland's first town, St. Mary's, was established in 1634 near where the Potomac River flows into the Chesapeake Bay.

While establishing a refuge for Catholics who were facing increasing persecution in Anglican England, the Calverts were also interested in creating profitable estates. To this end, and to avoid trouble with the British government, they also encouraged Protestant immigration.

The royal charter granted to the Calvert family had a mixture of feudal and modern elements. On the one hand, they had the power to create manorial estates. On the other, they could only make laws with the consent of freemen (property holders). They found that in order to attract settlers— and make a profit from their holdings—they had to offer people farms, not just tenancy on the manorial estates. The number of independent farms grew in consequence, and their owners demanded a voice in the affairs of the colony. Maryland's first legislature met in 1635.

1. Henry Hudson sailed up the Hudson River in

    a. 1609.
    b. 1617.
    c. 1620.
    d. 1624.

2. A fort was built where Albany now stands in

    a. 1609.
    b. 1617.
    c. 1620.
    d. 1624.

3. Manhattan was purchased in

    a. 1609.
    b. 1617.
    c. 1620.
    d. 1624.

4. At first, the Dutch were mainly interested in

    a. hunting and fishing.
    b. farming.
    c. feudal estates.
    d. furs.

5. The patroon system was set up by the Dutch government to

    a. attract settlers.
    b. grant land.
    c. grant privileges.
    d. earn rent.

6. New Sweden did **not**

    a. become part of New Netherland.
    b. establish itself along the Delaware.
    c. become part of Delaware and Pennsylvania.
    d. survive for long.

7. Maryland failed to attract

    a. tenant farmers.
    b. Catholics.
    c. independent farmers.
    d. citizens wanting a voice in government.

18

COLONIAL-INDIAN RELATIONS

By 1640, the British had solid colonies established along the New England coast and the Chesapeake Bay. In between were the Dutch and the tiny Swedish community. To the west were the original Americans, the Indians.

Sometimes friendly, sometimes hostile, the eastern tribes were no longer strangers to the Europeans. Although Native Americans benefitted from access to new technology and trade, the disease and thirst for land that the early settlers also brought posed a serious challenge to the Indians' long-established way of life.

At first, trade with the European settlers brought advantages: knives, axes, weapons, cooking utensils, fishhooks, and a host of other goods. Those Indians who traded initially had significant advantage over rivals who did not.

In response to European demand, tribes such as the Iroquois began to devote more attention to fur trapping during the 17th century. Furs and pelts provided tribes the means to purchase colonial goods until late into the 18th century.

Early colonial-Indian relations were an uneasy mix of cooperation and conflict. On the one hand, there were the exemplary relations that prevailed during the first half century of Pennsylvania's existence. On the other were a long series of setbacks, skirmishes, and wars, which almost invariably resulted in an Indian defeat and further loss of land.

The first of the important Indian uprisings occurred in Virginia in 1622, when some 347 whites were killed, including a number of missionaries who had just recently come to Jamestown. The Pequot War followed in 1637, as local tribes tried to prevent settlement of the Connecticut River region.

In 1675, Phillip, the son of the chief who had made the original peace with the Pilgrims in 1621, attempted to unite the tribes of southern New England against further European encroachment of their lands. In the struggle, however, Phillip lost his life and many Indians were sold into servitude.

Almost five thousand kilometers to the west, the Pueblo Indians rose up against the Spanish missionaries five years later in the area around Taos, New Mexico. For the next dozen years, the Pueblo controlled their former land again, only to see the Spanish retake it. Some sixty years later, another Indian revolt took place when the Pima Indians clashed with the Spanish in what is now Arizona.

The steady influx of settlers into the backwoods regions of the eastern colonies disrupted Indian life. As more and more game was killed off, tribes were faced with the difficult choice of going hungry, going to war, or moving and coming into conflict with other tribes to the west.

The Iroquois, who inhabited the area below Lakes Ontario and Erie in northern New York and Pennsylvania, were more successful in resisting European advances. In 1570, five tribes joined to form the most democratic nation of its time, the "Ho-De-No-Sau-Nee," or League of the Iroquois. The League was run by a council made up of fifty representatives from each of the five member tribes. The council dealt with matters common to all the tribes, but it had no say in how the free and equal tribes ran their day-to-day affairs. No tribe was allowed to make war by itself. The council passed laws to deal with crimes such as murder.

The League was a strong power in the 1600s and 1700s. It traded furs with the British and sided with them against the French in the war for the dominance of America between 1754 and 1763. The British might not have won that war without the support of the League of the Iroquois.

The League stayed strong until the American Revolution. Then, for the first time, the council could not reach a unanimous decision on whom to support. Member tribes made their own decisions, some fighting with the British, some with the colonists, some remaining neutral. As a result, everyone fought against the Iroquois. Their losses were great and the League never recovered.

1. In trading with Europeans, Indians provided

   a. knives and axes.
   b. fishhooks.
   c. furs and pelts.
   d. cooking utensils.

2. Relations between Indians and Europeans were most peaceful in

   a. Virginia.
   b. New England.
   c. Pennsylvania.
   d. New Mexico.

3. The Iroquois confederation united in favor of the British in the

   a. French and Indian War.
   b. Pequot War.
   c. King Phillips War.
   d. American Revolution.

SECOND GENERATION OF BRITISH COLONIES

The religious and civil conflict in England in the mid-17th century limited immigration, as well as the attention the mother country paid the fledgling American colonies.

In part to provide for the defense measures England was neglecting, the Massachusetts Bay, Plymouth, Connecticut, and New Haven colonies formed the New England Confederation in 1643. It was the European colonists' first attempt at regional unity.

The early history of the British settlers reveals a good deal of contention—religious and political—as groups vied for power and position among themselves and their neighbors. Maryland, in particular, suffered from the bitter religious rivalries afflicting England during the era of Oliver Cromwell. One of the casualties was the state's Toleration Act, which was revoked in the 1650s. It was soon reinstated, however, along with the religious freedom it guaranteed.

In 1675, Bacon's Rebellion, the first significant revolt against royal authority, broke out in the colonies. The original spark was a clash between Virginia frontiersmen and the Susquehannock Indians, but it soon pitted the common farmer against the wealth and privilege of the large planters and Virginia's governor, William Berkeley.

The small farmers, embittered by low tobacco prices and hard living conditions, rallied around Nathaniel Bacon, a recent arrival from England. Berkeley refused to grant Bacon a commission to conduct Indian raids, but he did agree to call new elections to the House of Burgesses, which had remained unchanged since 1661.

Defying Berkeley's orders, Bacon led an attack against the friendly Ocaneechee tribe, nearly wiping them out. Returning to Jamestown in September 1676, he burned it, forcing Berkeley to flee. Most of the state was now under Bacon's control. His victory was short-lived, however; he died of a fever the following month. Without Bacon, the rebellion soon lost its vitality. Berkeley reestablished his authority and hanged twenty-three of Bacon's followers.

With the restoration of King Charles II in 1660, the British once again turned their attentions to North America. Within a brief span, the first European settlements were established in the Carolinas and the Dutch driven out of New Netherland. New proprietary colonies were established in New York, New Jersey, Delaware, and Pennsylvania.

The Dutch settlements had, as a general matter, been ruled by autocratic governors appointed in Europe. Over the years, the local population had become estranged from them. As a result, when the British colonists began encroaching on Dutch lands in Long Island and Manhattan, the unpopular governor was unable to rally the population to their defense. New Netherland fell in 1664. The terms of the capitulation, however, were mild: the Dutch settlers were able to retain their property and worship as they pleased.

As early as the 1650s, the Ablemarle Sound region off the coast of what is now northern North Carolina was inhabited by settlers trickling down from Virginia. The first proprietary governor arrived in 1664. A remote area even today, Ablemarle's first town was not established until the arrival of a group of French Huguenots in 1704.

In 1670, the first settlers, drawn from New England and the Caribbean island of Barbados, arrived in what is now Charleston, South Carolina. An elaborate system of government, to which the British philosopher John Locke contributed, was prepared for the new colony. One of its prominent features was a failed attempt to create a hereditary nobility. One of the colony's least appealing aspects was the early trade in Indian slaves. Within time, however, timber, rice, and indigo gave the colony a worthier economic base.

Massachusetts Bay was the only colony driven by religious motives. In 1681, William Penn, a wealthy Quaker and friend of Charles II, received a large tract of land west of the Delaware River, which became known as Pennsylvania. To help populate it, Penn actively recruited a host of religious dissenters from England and the continent—Quakers, Mennonites, Amish, Moravians, and Baptists.

When Penn arrived the following year, there were already Dutch, Swedish, and English settlers living along the Delaware River. It was there he founded Philadelphia, the "City of Brotherly Love."

In keeping with his faith, Penn was motivated by a sense of equality not often found in other American colonies at the time. Thus, women in Pennsylvania had rights long before they did in other parts of America. Penn and his deputies also paid considerable attention to the colony's relations with the Delaware Indians, ensuring that they were paid for any land the Europeans settled on.

Georgia was settled in 1732, the last of the thirteen colonies to be established. Lying close to, if not actually inside the boundaries of Spanish Florida, the region was viewed as a buffer against Spanish incursion. But it had another unique quality: the man charged with Georgia's fortifications, General James Oglethorpe, was a reformer who deliberately set out to create a refuge where the poor and former prisoners would be given new opportunities.

Men and women with little active interest in a new life in America were often induced to make the move to the New World by the skillful persuasion of promoters. William Penn, for example, publicized the opportunities awaiting newcomers to the Pennsylvania colony. Judges and prison authorities offered convicts a chance to migrate to colonies like Georgia instead of serving prison sentences.

However, few colonists could finance the cost of passage for themselves and their families to make a start in the new land. In some cases, ships' captains received large rewards from the sale of service contracts for poor migrants, called "indentured servants," and every method from extravagant promises to actual kidnapping was used to take on as many passengers as their vessels could hold.

In other cases, the expenses of transportation and maintenance were paid by colonizing agencies like the Virginia or Massachusetts Bay Companies. In return, indentured servants agreed to work for the agencies as contract laborers, usually for four to seven years. Free at the end of this term, they would be given "freedom dues," sometimes including a small tract of land.

It has been estimated that half the settlers living in the colonies south of New England came to America under this system. Although most of them fulfilled their obligations faithfully, some ran away from their employers. Nevertheless, many of them were eventually able to secure land and set up homesteads, either in the colonies in which they had originally settled or in neighboring ones. No social stigma was attached to a family that had its beginning in America under this semi-bondage. Every colony had its share of leaders who were former indentured servants.

There was one very important exception to this pattern: African slaves. The first blacks were brought to Virginia in 1619, just twelve years after the founding of Jamestown. Initially, many were regarded as indentured servants who could earn their freedom. By the 1660s, however, as the demand for plantation labor in the southern colonies grew, the institution of slavery began to harden around them, and Africans were brought to America in shackles for a lifetime of involuntary servitude.

The first American literature is generally considered to be certain accounts of discoveries and explorations in America. They frequently display the style characteristic of contemporary Elizabethan writers (1558–1603). Captain John Smith, the first great figure in American letters, wrote *The General Historie of Virginia, New England, and the Summer Isles* (1624). Many writings eloquently provided a religious explanation for every event. Such notable works include *History of Plymouth Plantation* by William Bradford. He was an early governor of Plymouth Colony. A similar text was *The History of New England* by John Winthrop, the earliest governor of the Massachusetts Bay Colony. Other early American writings are accounts of Native American wars and of captivities. The most noteworthy colonial poets were Anne Bradstreet, "The Tenth Muse Lately Sprung Up in America," 1650; Edward Taylor; and Michael Wigglesworth, "The Day of Doom, 1662."

1. The New England Confederation of 1643 united _____ colonies.

    a. two
    b. three
    c. four
    d. five

22

2. Nathaniel Bacon and his followers were upset over all of the following **except**

    a. Indian attacks.
    b. low tobacco prices.
    c. high pork prices.
    c. the wealth and privileges of large planters.

3. Bacon's revolt of 1675

    a. failed immediately.
    b. was a short-term success.
    c. was a long-term success.
    d. chased William Berkeley back to England.

4. With the restoration of Charles II in England, the British established themselves in all of the following areas **except**

    a. Florida.
    b. the Carolinas.
    c. New York and New Jersey.
    d. Pennsylvania and Delaware.

5. _____ fell to the British in 1664 without a battle.

    a. New Sweden
    b. New Netherland
    c. Charleston, South Carolina
    d. Delaware

6. South Carolina failed to establish

    a. trade in Indian slaves.
    b. heredity nobility.
    c. trade in timber.
    d. trade in rice and indigo.

7. Even before William Penn arrived, all of the following had settled along the Delaware River **except** the

    a. Dutch
    b. Swedish
    c. English
    d. French Huguenots

8. William Penn welcomed all of the following **except**

    a. Quakers.
    b. Mennonites.
    c. Catholics.
    d. Amish.

9. Which of the following did **not** offer refuge to outcasts of one land or another?

   a. Rhode Island.
   b. Georgia.
   c. Virginia.
   d. Pennsylvania.

10. Half the settlers of the following states **except** _____ were probably indentured servants.

   a. New York
   b. Pennsylvania
   c. Virginia
   d. Connecticut

11. The first African slaves came to _____ in 1619.

   a. Virginia
   b. Georgia
   c. Delaware
   d. New Jersey

Chapter 2
Questions for Further Research

1. Describe how the earliest Europeans in the Americas interacted with Native Americans.

2. Describe how political institutions emerged in the North American colonies.

3. Describe how religious freedom emerged in the North American colonies.

4. Describe how the values and institutions of European economic life took root in the colonies.

5. Describe how slavery reshaped European and African life in the Americas.

6. Compare English, French, and Dutch motives for exploration and colonization with those of the Spanish.

7. Describe the arrival of Africans in the English colonies in the 17th century and the rapid increase of slave importation in the 18th century.

8. Compare the first settlers who established Jamestown, Plymouth, and Philadelphia. What were their backgrounds, reasons for coming, resources, occupational skills, leadership qualities, and ability to work together?

9. Contrast and compare the early English settlements with a Spanish settlement (e.g., St. Augustine or Santa Fe) and a French settlement (e.g., Quebec or New Orleans). How did the people who came to these settlements differ from those in the English colonies?

10. Compare the growth of the European colonies in the two centuries following their founding. What new groups arrived, voluntarily in the case of European colonists, involuntarily in the case of Africans forced into indentured servitude and slavery? How did the colonies change as their population grew?

11. Describe family life, gender roles, and women's rights in colonial North America.

12. Explain how and why family and community life differed in various regions of colonial North America.

13. Compare how English settlers interacted with Native Americans in New England, mid-Atlantic, Chesapeake, and lower South colonies.

14. How did various Native American societies change as a result of the expanding European settlements and how were they influenced by European societies?

15. Describe and analyze the significance of colonial wars before 1754.

16. Compare Native American and European views of the land.

17. Compare William Penn's friendly relations with the Lenni Lenape and Susquehannocks with the wars between the colonial settlers and the Powhatans in Virginia (1622) and the Pequots in Massachusetts (1637).

18. Was conflict unavoidable in European relationships with the Native Americans?

19. How were Native Americans and European societies in North America influenced by one another?

20. In what ways did the early settlers in Massachusetts and Virginia depend on the skills and assistance of Native Americans in order to survive?

21. In what ways did trade benefit Native Americans and Europeans and foster alliances, but also change traditional patterns of Native American life in ways that were harmful?

22. Describe English colonists who opposed prevailing policies toward Native Americans and demonstrated that alternatives to hostility existed.

23. How did such individuals as Roger Williams, William Penn, and John Eliot differ in their actions toward Native Americans from most of their countrymen, and with what results?

24. What explains the generally friendly relations in Rhode Island and Quaker Pennsylvania?

25. Why were French relations with the Hurons, Ottawas, and Algonkians among the friendliest on the continent?

26. Compare how early colonies were established and governed.

27. Describe the background and significance of the Mayflower Compact.

28. Describe the religious diversity between and within the colonies.

29. Explain why the Puritans came to America, how Puritanism shaped New England communities and how Puritanism changed during the 17th century.

30. Trace and explain the evolution of religious freedom in the English colonies.

31. Describe Anne Hutchinson's history and trial. Evaluate her behavior, and evaluate the justice of her banishment from the Massachusetts Bay Colony.

32. Compare the treatment of dissenters in various colonies such as Puritan Massachusetts, Anglican Virginia, and Quaker Pennsylvania.

33. Why did Puritans immigrate in search of religious freedom and then deny it to others?

34. What did Roger Williams mean by separation of church and state? Do we have the same meaning of separation of church and state today?

CHAPTER 3
The Colonial Period

NEW PEOPLES

Most settlers who came to America in the 17th century were English, but there were also Dutch, Swedes, and Germans in the middle region, a few French Huguenots in South Carolina and elsewhere, slaves from Africa—primarily in the South—and a scattering of Spaniards, Italians, and Portuguese throughout the colonies.

After 1680, England ceased to be the chief source of immigration. Thousands of refugees fled continental Europe to escape the path of war. Many left their homelands to avoid the poverty induced by government oppression and absentee-landlordism.

By 1690, the American population had risen to a quarter of a million. From then on, it doubled every twenty-five years until, in 1775, it numbered more than two and a half million.

Although a family could move from Massachusetts to Virginia or from South Carolina to Pennsylvania without major readjustment, distinctions between individual colonies were marked. They were even more so between the three regional groupings of colonies.

1. Before 1680, most of the settlers in America were

   a. African slaves.
   b. Germans.
   b. English.
   c. Spanish.

2. The population in 1690 was

   a. 250,000.
   b. 2.5 million.
   c. 25 million.
   d. 250 million.

26

3. After 1680, most of the immigrants were

   a. slaves.
   b. English.
   c. from the European Continent.
   d. Italians and Portuguese.

NEW ENGLAND

New England in the northeast has generally thin, stony soil, relatively little level land, and long winters, making it difficult to make a living from farming. Turning to other pursuits, the New Englanders harnessed water power and established grain mills and sawmills. Good stands of timber encouraged shipbuilding. Excellent harbors promoted trade, and the sea became a source of great wealth. In Massachusetts, the cod industry alone quickly furnished a basis for prosperity.

With the bulk of the early settlers living in villages and towns around the harbors, many New Englanders carried on some kind of trade or business. Common pastureland and woodlots served the needs of townspeople, who worked small farms nearby. Compactness made possible the village school, the village church, and the village or town hall, where citizens met to discuss matters of common interest.

The Massachusetts Bay Colony continued to expand its commerce. From the middle of the 17th century onward, it grew prosperous. Boston became one of America's greatest ports.

Oak timber for ships' hulls, tall pines for spars and masts, and pitch for the seams of ships came from the northeastern forests. Building their own vessels and sailing them to ports all over the world, the shipmasters of Massachusetts Bay laid the foundation for a trade that was to grow steadily in importance. By the end of the colonial period, one-third of all vessels under the British flag were built in New England. Fish, ships' stores, and wooden ware swelled the exports.

New England shippers soon discovered, too, that rum and slaves were profitable commodities. One of the most enterprising—if unsavory—trading practices of the time was the so-called "triangular trade." Merchants and shippers would purchase slaves off the coast of Africa for New England rum, then sell the slaves in the West Indies where they would buy molasses to bring home for sale to the local rum producers.

1. Farmers in New England were aided by

   a. poor soil.
   b. lack of level land.
   c. long winters.
   d. common pastureland and woodland.

2. Shipbuilders relied on New England's resources for all of the following **except**

   a. molasses.
   b. oak for hulls.
   c. pine for masts.
   d. pitch.

3. New Englanders did **not**

    a. gather in small villages.
    b. farm large plantations.
    c. sell many ships to England.
    d. engage in triangular trade.

4. The triangular trade involved all of the following **except**

    a. rum.
    b. slaves.
    c. fish.
    d. molasses.

5. New England towns typically did **not** have

    a. access to the sea.
    b. a village school, church, and hall.
    c. traders, businessmen, and small farmers.
    d. elaborate stone and brick houses.

THE WITCHES OF SALEM

In 1692, a group of adolescent girls in Salem Village, Massachusetts, became subject to strange fits after hearing tales told by a West Indian slave. When they were questioned, they accused several women of being witches who were tormenting them. The townspeople were appalled, but not surprised; belief in witchcraft was widespread throughout 17th-century America and Europe.

What happened next—although an isolated event in American history—provides a vivid window into the social and psychological world of Puritan New England. Town officials convened a court to hear the charges of witchcraft, and swiftly convicted and executed a tavernkeeper, Bridget Bishop. Within a month, five other women had been convicted and hanged.

Nevertheless, the hysteria grew, in large measure because the court permitted witnesses to testify that they had seen the accused as spirits or in visions. By its very nature, such "spectral evidence" was especially dangerous, because it could be neither verified nor subject to objective examination. By the fall of 1692, more than twenty victims, including several men, had been executed and more than one hundred others were in jail—among them some of the town's most prominent citizens. But now the hysteria threatened to spread beyond Salem, and ministers throughout the colony called for an end to the trials. The governor of the colony agreed and dismissed the court. Those still in jail were later acquitted or given reprieves.

The Salem witch trials have long fascinated Americans. On a psychological level, most historians agree that Salem Village, in 1692, was seized by a kind of public hysteria, fueled by a genuine belief in the existence of witchcraft. They point out that while some of the girls may have been acting, many responsible adults became caught up in the frenzy as well.

Even more revealing is a closer analysis of the identities of the accused and the accusers. Salem Village, like much of colonial New England at that time, was undergoing an economic and political transition from a largely agrarian, Puritan-dominated community to a more commercial, secular society. Many of the accusers were representatives of a traditional way of life tied to farming and the church, whereas a number of the accused witches were members of the rising commercial

28

class of small shopkeepers and tradesmen. Salem's obscure struggle for social and political power between older traditional groups and a newer commercial class was one repeated in communities throughout American history. However, it took a bizarre and deadly detour when its citizens were swept up by the conviction that the devil was loose in their homes.

The Salem witch trials also serve as a dramatic parable of the deadly consequences of making sensational, but false, charges. Indeed, a frequent term in political debate for making false accusations against a large number of people is "witch hunt."

1. The Salem witch trials occurred in

    a. 1612.
    b. 1692.
    c. 1912.
    d. 1962.

2. The first accusations were made by

    a. adolescent girls.
    b. a West Indian slave.
    c. a tavernkeeper.
    d. ministers.

3. The trials ended only after

    a. 100 victims were charged.
    b. prominent citizens were reprieved.
    c. the governor was accused.
    d. the hysteria threatened to spread beyond Salem.

4. All of the following were factors in the trials **except**

    a. widespread belief in witchcraft.
    b. tensions between ways of life.
    c. religious discrimination.
    d. spectral evidence.

THE MIDDLE COLONIES

Society in the middle colonies was far more varied, cosmopolitan, and tolerant than in New England. In many ways, Pennsylvania and Delaware owed their initial success to William Penn.

Under his guidance, Pennsylvania functioned smoothly and grew rapidly. By 1685, its population was almost nine thousand. The heart of the colony was Philadelphia, a city soon to be known for its broad, tree-shaded streets, substantial brick and stone houses, and busy docks. By the end of the colonial period, nearly a century later, thirty thousand people lived there, representing many languages, creeds, and trades. Their talent for successful business enterprise made the city one of the thriving centers of colonial America.

Though the Quakers dominated in Philadelphia, elsewhere in Pennsylvania others were well represented. Germans became the colony's most skillful farmers. Important, too, were cottage industries such as weaving, shoemaking, cabinetmaking, and other crafts.

29

Pennsylvania was also the principal gateway into the New World for the Scots-Irish, who moved into the colony in the early 18th century. "Bold and indigent strangers," as one Pennsylvania official called them, they hated the English and were suspicious of all government. The Scots-Irish tended to settle in the backcountry, where they cleared land and lived by hunting and subsistence farming.

As mixed as the people were in Pennsylvania, New York best illustrated the polyglot nature of America. By 1646, the population along the Hudson River included Dutch, French, Danes, Norwegians, Swedes, English, Scots, Irish, Germans, Poles, Bohemians, Portuguese, and Italians—the forerunners of millions to come.

The Dutch continued to exercise an important social and economic influence on the New York region long after the fall of New Netherland and their integration into the British colonial system. Their sharp-stepped, gable roofs became a permanent part of the city's architecture, and their merchants gave Manhattan much of its original bustling, commercial atmosphere.

1. The most varied population in America lived in

    a. Delaware.
    b. New Jersey.
    c. Pennsylvania.
    d. New York.

2. The Scots-Irish did **not**

    a. hate the English.
    b. settle in and around Philadelphia.
    c. live by hunting and subsistence farming.
    d. live in the backcountry.

3. The Pennsylvania Dutch were actually "Deutsche," or

    a. Germans.
    b. Swedes.
    c. Quakers.
    d. Dutch.

4. The _____ remained an integral part of New York's commerce and society.

    a. Dutch
    b. French
    c. Danes
    d. Norwegians

THE SOUTHERN COLONIES

In contrast to New England and the middle colonies were the predominantly rural southern settlements: Virginia, Maryland, North and South Carolina, and Georgia.

By the late 17th century, Virginia's and Maryland's economic and social structure rested on the great planters and the yeoman farmers. The planters of the tidewater region, supported by slave labor, held most of the political power and the best land. They built great houses, adopted an aristocratic way of life, and kept in touch as best they could with the world of culture overseas.

30

At the same time, yeoman farmers, who worked smaller tracts of land, sat in popular assemblies and found their way into political office. Their outspoken independence was a constant warning to the oligarchy of planters not to encroach too far upon the rights of free men.

Charleston, South Carolina, became the leading port and trading center of the South. There the settlers quickly learned to combine agriculture and commerce, and the marketplace became a major source of prosperity. Dense forests also brought revenue: lumber, tar, and resin from the longleaf pine provided some of the best shipbuilding materials in the world. Not bound to a single crop as was Virginia, North and South Carolina also produced and exported rice and indigo, a blue dye obtained from native plants, which was used in coloring fabric. By 1750, more than 100,000 people lived in the two colonies of North and South Carolina.

In the southernmost colonies, as everywhere else, population growth in the backcountry had special significance. German immigrants and Scots-Irish, unwilling to live in the original tidewater settlements where English influence was strong, pushed inland. Those who could not secure fertile land along the coast, or who had exhausted the lands they held, found the hills farther west a bountiful refuge. Although their hardships were enormous, restless settlers kept coming, and by the 1730s they were pouring into the Shenandoah Valley of Virginia. Soon the interior was dotted with farms.

Living on the edge of the Indian country, frontier families built cabins, cleared tracts in the wilderness, and cultivated maize and wheat. The men wore leather made from the skin of deer or sheep, known as buckskin; the women wore garments of cloth they spun at home. Their food consisted of venison, wild turkey, and fish. They had their own amusements— great barbecues, dances, housewarmings for newly married couples, shooting matches, and contests for making quilted blankets. Quilts remain an American tradition today.

1. Virginia plantation owners and yeoman farmers both

   a. lived in the tidewater region.
   b. relied on slaves or labor.
   c. grew tobacco.
   d. adapted an aristocratic way of life.

2. Virginia plantation owners and yeoman farmers both

   a. worked small tracts of land.
   b. sat in popular assemblies.
   c. lived inland.
   d. held political power.

3. North and South Carolina exported all of the following **except**

   a. tea.
   b. lumber, tar, and resin.
   c. rice.
   d. indigo.

4. The principal port of the southern colonies was

   a. Boston, Massachusetts.
   b. New York, New York.
   c. Philadelphia, Pennsylvania.
   d. Charleston, South Carolina.

5. By the 1730s, German and Scots-Irish immigrants had

    a. taken over tidewaters plantations.
    b. gathered together in southern cities.
    c. settled in the southern backcountry.
    d. adopted eastern clothes and amusement.

SOCIETY, SCHOOLS, AND CULTURE

A significant factor deterring the emergence of a powerful aristocratic or gentry class in the colonies was the fact that anyone in an established colony could choose to find a new home on the frontier. Thus, time after time, dominant tidewater figures were obliged, by the threat of a mass exodus to the frontier, to liberalize political policies, land-grant requirements, and religious practices. This movement into the foothills was of tremendous import for the future of America.

Of equal significance for the future were the foundations of American education and culture established during the colonial period. Harvard College was founded in 1636 in Cambridge, Massachusetts. Near the end of the century, the College of William and Mary was established in Virginia. A few years later, the Collegiate School of Connecticut, later to become Yale College, was chartered. But even more noteworthy was the growth of a school system maintained by governmental authority. The Puritan emphasis on reading directly from the Scriptures underscored the importance of literacy.

In 1647, the Massachusetts Bay Colony enacted the "ye olde deluder Satan" Act, requiring every town having more than fifty families to establish a grammar school (a Latin school to prepare students for college). Shortly thereafter, all the other New England colonies, except Rhode Island, followed its example.

The first immigrants in New England brought their own little libraries and continued to import books from London. And as early as the 1680s, Boston booksellers were doing a thriving business in works of classical literature, history, politics, philosophy, science, theology, and belles-lettres. In 1639, the first printing press in the English colonies and the second in North America was installed at Harvard College.

The first school in Pennsylvania was begun in 1683. It taught reading, writing, and keeping of accounts. Thereafter, in some fashion, every Quaker community provided for the elementary teaching of its children. More advanced training—in classical languages, history, and literature—was offered at the Friends Public School, which still operates in Philadelphia as the William Penn Charter School. The school was free to the poor, but parents who could were required to pay tuition.

In Philadelphia, numerous private schools with no religious affiliation taught languages, mathematics, and natural science; there were also night schools for adults. Women were not entirely overlooked, but their educational opportunities were limited to training in activities that could be conducted in the home. Private teachers instructed the daughters of prosperous Philadelphians in French, music, dancing, painting, singing, grammar, and sometimes even bookkeeping.

In the 18th century, the intellectual and cultural development of Pennsylvania reflected, in large measure, the vigorous personalities of two men: James Logan and Benjamin Franklin. Logan was secretary of the colony, and it was in his fine library that young Franklin found the latest scientific works. In 1745, Logan erected a building for his collection and bequeathed both building and books to the city.

Franklin contributed even more to the intellectual activity of Philadelphia. He formed a debating club that became the embryo of the American Philosophical Society. His endeavors also led to the founding of a public academy that later developed into the University of Pennsylvania. He was a prime mover in the establishment of a subscription library, which he called "the mother of all North American subscription libraries."

In the southern colonies, wealthy planters and merchants imported private tutors from Ireland or Scotland to teach their children. Others sent their children to school in England. Having these other opportunities, the upper classes in the Tidewater were not interested in supporting public education. In addition, the diffusion of farms and plantations made the formation of community schools difficult. There were a few endowed free schools in Virginia; the Syms School was founded in 1647 and the Eaton School emerged in 1659.

The desire for learning did not stop at the borders of established communities, however. On the frontier, the Scots-Irish, though living in primitive cabins, were firm devotees of scholarship, and they made great efforts to attract learned ministers to their settlements.

Literary production in the colonies was largely confined to NewEngland. Here attention concentrated on religious subjects. Sermons were the most common products of the press. A famous Puritan minister, the Reverend Cotton Mather, wrote some four hundred works. His masterpiece, *Magnalia Christi Americana*, presented the pageant of New England's history. But the most popular single work of the day was the Reverend Michael Wigglesworth's long poem, "The Day of Doom," which described the last judgment in terrifying terms.

In 1704, Cambridge, Massachusetts, launched the colonies' first successful newspaper. By 1745, there were twenty-two newspapers being published throughout the colonies.

In New York, an important step in establishing the principle of freedom of the press took place with the case of Johann Peter Zenger, whose *New York Weekly Journal*, begun in 1733, represented the opposition to the government. After two years of publication, the colonial governor could no longer tolerate Zenger's satirical barbs and had him thrown into prison on a charge of seditious libel. Zenger continued to edit his paper from jail during his nine-month trial, which excited intense interest throughout the colonies. Andrew Hamilton, the prominent lawyer who defended Zenger, argued that the charges printed by Zenger were true and hence not libelous. The jury returned a verdict of not guilty and Zenger went free.

The prosperity of the towns, which prompted fears that the devil was luring society into pursuit of worldly gain, produced a religious reaction in the 1730s that came to be known as the Great Awakening. Its inspiration came from two sources: George Whitefield, a Wesleyan revivalist who arrived from England in 1739, and Jonathan Edwards, who originally served in the Congregational Church in Northampton, Massachusetts.

Whitefield began a religious revival in Philadelphia and then moved on to New England. He enthralled audiences of up to twenty thousand people at a time with histrionic displays, gestures, and emotional oratory. Religious turmoil swept throughout New England and the middle colonies as ministers left established churches to preach the revival.

Among those influenced by Whitefield was Edwards, and the Great Awakening reached its culmination in 1741 with his sermon "Sinners in the Hands of an Angry God." Edwards did not

33

engage in theatrics, but delivered his sermons in a quiet, thoughtful manner. He stressed that the established churches sought to deprive Christianity of its emotional content. His magnum opus, *Of Freedom of Will* (1754), attempted to reconcile Calvinism with the Enlightenment.

The Great Awakening gave rise to evangelical denominations and the spirit of revivalism, which continue to play significant roles in American religious and cultural life. It weakened the status of the established clergy and provoked believers to rely on their own conscience. Perhaps most important, it led to the proliferation of sects and denominations, which in turn encouraged general acceptance of the principle of religious toleration.

1. The first American college was in

   a. Massachusetts.
   b. Virginia.
   c. Connecticut.
   d. Rhode Island.

2. The first colony to require public education was

   a. Massachusetts.
   b. Virginia.
   c. Connecticut.
   d. Rhode Island.

3. The first printing press in an English colony was in

   a. Massachusetts.
   b. Virginia.
   c. Connecticut.
   d. Rhode Island.

4. Benjamin Franklin was instrumental in founding all of the following **except**

   a. a scientific library.
   b. a subscription library.
   c. an American Philosophical Association.
   d. the University of Pennsylvania.

5. The first newspaper in the colonies was published

   a. on the frontier.
   b. in the southern colonies.
   c. in Philadelphia, Pennsylvania.
   d. in Cambridge, Massachusetts.

6. Johann Peter Zenger won an important case that helped establish

   a. Andrew Hamilton's reputation.
   b. the colonial governor's reputation.
   c. freedom of the press.
   d. a right to privacy.

34

7. The Great Awakening was started by
   a. Cotton Mather.
   b. Michael Wigglesworth.
   c. George Whitefield.
   d. Jonathan Edwards.

EMERGENCE OF COLONIAL GOVERNMENT

In all phases of colonial development, a striking feature was the lack of controlling influence by the English government. All colonies except Georgia emerged as companies of shareholders, or as feudal proprietorships stemming from charters granted by the Crown. The fact that the king had transferred his immediate sovereignty over the New World settlements to stock companies and proprietors did not, of course, mean that the colonists in America were necessarily free of outside control. Under the terms of the Virginia Company charter, for example, full governmental authority was vested in the company itself. Nevertheless, the crown expected that the company would be resident in England. Inhabitants of Virginia, then, would have no more voice in their government than if the king himself had retained absolute rule.

For their part, the colonies had never thought of themselves as subservient. Rather, they considered themselves chiefly as commonwealths or states, much like England itself, having only a loose association with the authorities in London. In one way or another, exclusive rule from the outside withered away. The colonists—inheritors of the traditions of the Englishman's long struggle for political liberty—incorporated concepts of freedom into Virginia's first charter. It provided that English colonists were to exercise all liberties, franchises, and immunities "as if they had been abiding and born within this our Realm of England." They were, then, to enjoy the benefits of the Magna Carta and the common law. In 1618, the Virginia Company issued instructions to its appointed governor providing that free inhabitants of the plantations should elect representatives to join with the governor and an appointive council in passing ordinances for the welfare of the colony.

These measures proved to be some of the most far-reaching in the entire colonial period. From then on, it was generally accepted that the colonists had a right to participate in their own government. In most instances, the king, in making future grants, provided in the charter that the freemen of the colony should have a voice in legislation affecting them. Thus, charters awarded to the Calverts in Maryland, William Penn in Pennsylvania, the proprietors in North and South Carolina, and the proprietors in New Jersey specified that legislation should be enacted with "the consent of the freemen."

In New England, for many years, there was even more complete self-government than in the other colonies. Aboard the *Mayflower*, the Pilgrims adopted an instrument for government called the "Mayflower Compact" to "combine ourselves together into a civil body politic for our better ordering and preservation . . . and by virtue hereof [to] enact, constitute, and frame such just and equal laws, ordinances, acts, constitutions, and offices . . . as shall be thought most meet and convenient for the general good of the colony . . . "

Although there was no legal basis for the Pilgrims to establish a system of self-government, the action was not contested and, under the compact, the Plymouth settlers were able for many years to conduct their own affairs without outside interference.

A similar situation developed in the Massachusetts Bay Company, which had been given the right to govern itself. Thus, full authority rested in the hands of persons residing in the colony. At first, the dozen or so original members of the company who had come to America attempted to rule autocratically. However, the other colonists soon demanded a voice in public affairs and indicated that refusal would lead to a mass migration.

Faced with this threat, the company members yielded and control of the government passed to elected representatives. Subsequently, other New England colonies—such as Connecticut and Rhode Island—also succeeded in becoming self-governing simply by asserting that they were beyond any governmental authority, and then setting up their own political system modeled after that of the Pilgrims at Plymouth.

In only two cases was the self-government provision omitted. These were New York, which was granted to Charles II's brother, the Duke of York (later to become King James II); and Georgia, which was granted to a group of "trustees." In both instances, the provisions for governance were short-lived, for the colonists demanded legislative representation so insistently that the authorities soon yielded.

Eventually, most colonies became royal colonies, but in the mid-17th century, the English were too distracted by the Civil War (1642–1649) and Oliver Cromwell's Puritan Commonwealth and Protectorate to pursue an effective colonial policy. After the restoration of Charles II and the Stuart dynasty in 1660, England had more opportunity to attend to colonial administration. Even then, however, it was inefficient and lacked a coherent plan, and the colonies were left largely to their own devices.

The remoteness afforded by a vast ocean also made control of the colonies difficult. Added to this was the character of life itself in early America. From countries limited in space and dotted with populous towns, the settlers had come to a land of seemingly unending reach. On such a continent, natural conditions promoted a tough individualism, as people became used to making their own decisions. Government penetrated the backcountry only slowly, and conditions of anarchy often prevailed on the frontier.

Yet, the assumption of self-government in the colonies did not go entirely unchallenged. In the 1670s, the Lords of Trade and Plantations, a royal committee established to enforce the mercantile system on the colonies, moved to annul the Massachusetts Bay charter, because the colony was resisting the government's economic policy. James II in 1685 approved a proposal to create a Dominion of New England and place colonies south through New Jersey under its jurisdiction, thereby tightening the Crown's control over the whole region. A royal governor, Sir Edmund Andros, levied taxes by executive order, implemented a number of other harsh measures, and jailed those who resisted.

When news of the Glorious Revolution (1688–1689) that deposed James II reached Boston, the population rebelled and imprisoned Andros. Under a new charter, Massachusetts and Plymouth were united for the first time in 1691 as the royal colony of Massachusetts Bay. The other colonies that had come under the Dominion of New England quickly reinstalled their previous governments.

The Glorious Revolution had other positive effects on the colonies. The Bill of Rights and Toleration Act of 1689 affirmed freedom of worship for Christians and enforced limits on the Crown. Equally important, John Locke's *Second Treatise on Government* (1690) set forth a theory of government based not on divine right but on contract, and contended that the people—endowed with natural rights of life, liberty, and property—had the right to rebel when governments violated these natural rights.

Colonial politics in the early 18th century resembled English politics in the 17th. The Glorious Revolution affirmed the supremacy of Parliament, but colonial governors sought to exercise powers in the colonies that the king had lost in England. The colonial assemblies, aware of events in England, attempted to assert their "rights" and "liberties." By the early 18th century, the colonial legislatures held two significant powers similar to those held by the English Parliament: the right to vote on taxes and expenditures, and the right to initiate legislation rather than merely act on proposals of the governor.

The legislatures used these rights to check the power of royal governors and to pass other measures to expand their power and influence. The recurring clashes between governor and assembly worked increasingly to awaken the colonists to the divergence between American and English interests. In many cases, the royal authorities did not understand the importance of what the colonial assemblies were doing and simply neglected them. However, these acts established precedents and principles and eventually became part of the "constitution" of the colonies.

In this way, the colonial legislatures established the right of self-government. In time, the center of colonial administration shifted from London to the provincial capitals.

1. The only colony directly ruled at first by the English government was

    a. Massachusetts.
    b. Virginia.
    c. Pennsylvania.
    d. Georgia.

2. The first colonists considered themselves

    a. subservient to England.
    b. without any rights at all.
    c. only loosely affiliated with England.
    d. completely under England's authority.

3. Virginia's first charter

    a. denied all rights to colonists.
    b. granted them rights under the Magna Carta and English Common Law.
    c. prohibited elected representatives.
    d. permitted residents to elect a governor.

4. The charters of Maryland, Pennsylvania, New Jersey, and the Carolinas all provided for

    a. the election of a governor.
    b. the election of representatives to Parliament.
    c. the consent of freemen to legislation.
    d. taxation without representation.

5. The highest degree of self-governance was in

    a. New England.
    b. New York.
    c. Georgia.
    d. Florida.

6. The New England colonies first lost their freedom after the beginning of

    a. the Civil War of 1642–1649.
    b. Oliver Cromwell's Puritan Commonwealth and Protectorate.
    c. The Restoration of Charles II and the Stuarts in 1660.
    d. Charles II's brother, the Duke of York, became King James II.

7. New England, New York, and New Jersey were all placed under one royal governor,

    a. Oliver Cromwell.
    b. William of Orange.
    c. Sir Edmund Andros.
    d. James II.

8. Andros's governorship and the attempts to stifle colonial self-government ended with

    a. Oliver Cromwell.
    b. King James II.
    c. King Charles II.
    d. the Glorious Revolution (1688–1689).

9. The colonial residents consolidated their rights after 1690 despite

    a. the Bill of Rights and Toleration Act.
    b. John Locke's *Second Treatise on Government*.
    c. attempts by colonial governors to exercise greater power.
    d. the legislature's right to vote on taxes and expenditures.

10. The _____ were a decisive factor in establishing the right self-government and highlight conflicts between American and English interests.

    a. English Parliament
    b. colonial legislatures
    c. royal governors
    d. royal ministers

THE FRENCH AND INDIAN WAR

France and Britain engaged in a succession of wars in Europe and the Caribbean at several intervals in the 18th century. Though Britain secured certain advantages from them—primarily in the sugar-rich islands of the Caribbean—the struggles were generally indecisive, and France remained in a powerful position in North America at the beginning of the Seven Years' War in 1754.

By that time, France had established a strong relationship with a number of Indian tribes in Canada and along the Great Lakes, taken possession of the Mississippi River, and, by establishing a line of forts and trading posts, marked out a great crescent-shaped empire stretching from Quebec to New Orleans. Thus, the British were confined to the narrow belt east of the Appalachian Mountains. The French threatened not only the British Empire but the American colonists themselves, for in holding the Mississippi Valley, France could limit their westward expansion.

38

An armed clash took place in 1754 at Fort Duquesne, the site where Pittsburgh, Pennsylvania, is now located, between a band of French regulars and Virginia militiamen under the command of 22-year-old George Washington, a Virginia planter and surveyor.

In London, the Board of Trade attempted to deal with the conflict by calling a meeting of representatives from New York, Pennsylvania, Maryland, and the New England colonies. From June 19 to July 10, the Albany Congress, as it came to be known, met with the Iroquois at Albany, New York, in order to improve relations with them and secure their loyalty to the British.

The delegates also declared a union of the American colonies "absolutely necessary for their preservation," and adopted the Albany Plan of Union. Drafted by Benjamin Franklin, the plan provided that a president appointed by the king act with a grand council of delegates chosen by the assemblies, with each colony to be represented in proportion to its financial contributions to the general treasury. This organ would have charge of defense, Indian relations, and trade and settlement of the West, as well as having the power to levy taxes. However, none of the colonies accepted Franklin's plan, for none wished to surrender either the power of taxation or control over the development of the western lands to a central authority.

England's superior strategic position and her competent leadership ultimately brought victory in the Seven Years' War, only a modest portion of which was fought in the Western Hemisphere.

In the Peace of Paris, signed in 1763, France relinquished all of Canada, the Great Lakes, and the upper Mississippi Valley to the British. The dream of a French empire in North America was over.

Having triumphed over France, Britain was now compelled to face a problem that it had hitherto neglected—the governance of its empire. It was essential that London organize its now vast possessions to facilitate defense, reconcile the divergent interests of different areas and peoples, and distribute more evenly the cost of imperial administration.

In North America alone, British territories had more than doubled. To the narrow strip along the Atlantic coast had been added the vast expanse of Canada and the territory between the Mississippi River and the Allegheny Mountains, an empire in itself. A population that had been predominantly Protestant and English now included French-speaking Catholics from Quebec, and large numbers of partly Christianized Indians. Defense and administration of the new territories, as well as of the old, would require huge sums of money and increased personnel. The old colonial system was obviously inadequate to these tasks.

1. The French and their Indian allies threatened to stifle American expansion because they held

    a. the Carribean.
    b. Quebec and the St. Lawrence.
    c. the Ohio and Mississippi River valleys.
    d. Albany.

2. The first armed clash of the French and Indian War occurred when _____ led a band of militia men on an unprovoked attack on French soldiers near Fort Duquesne.

    a. George Washington
    b. Benjamin Franklin
    c. John Hancock
    d. John Adams

39

3. The Albany Congress

   a. rejected a union of American colonies.
   b. rejected a president appointed by the king.
   c. met with the Iroquois to improve relations.
   d. met with the Board of Trade in London.

4. Benjamin Franklin's Albany Plan of Union was rejected by

   a. the delegates.
   b. the Iroquois.
   c. the king.
   d. the colonies.

5. The French and Indian War was known in Europe as the

   a. Seven Years' War.
   b. English Civil War.
   c. Glorious Revolution.
   d. French Revolution.

6. The Peace of Paris in 1763

   a. was signed after the French won the war in Europe.
   b. was signed after the British won the war in North America.
   c. gave the French control of Canada and the Mississippi.
   d. gave the British control of Canada and the Mississippi.

Chapter 3
Questions for Further Research

1. Define mercantilism and explain how it influenced patterns of economic activity. Analyze the advantages and disadvantages of mercantilism for both England and its colonies.

2. Identify the major economic regions in the Americas and explain how labor systems shaped them.

3. Describe the crops, animal products, minerals, and other natural resources found in the New England, Middle Atlantic, and southern colonies.

4. Describe the economic relationships between the colonies, the Caribbean Islands, and England.

5. Compare the regions that produced sugar, rice, tobacco, timber, coffee, grains, fish, and minerals, and consider their value to the mother country.

6. Explain how environmental and human factors accounted for differences in the economies that developed in the colonies of New England, the mid-Atlantic, Chesapeake, and lower South.

7. Describe how the early Navigation Acts affected economic life in the colonies.

8. Compare the characteristics of free labor, indentured servitude, and chattel slavery, and describe where each was prevalent, and why.

9. Compare and contrast family farming in New England with plantation life in the Chesapeake and with small yeoman farming in the southern piedmont.

10. Describe the New England merchants' trading triangle and the goods and people regularly transported between the English colonies, West Indies, Africa, and Great Britain.

11. Describe the enslavement process and the "middle passage."

12. Describe laws enacted in Virginia and Maryland that helped institutionalize slavery. What rights were taken away from enslaved Africans? What restrictions were placed on white-black relations? How was slavery made perpetual and hereditary?

13. Describe the influence of African heritage on slave life in the colonies.

14. How did enslaved Africans draw upon their heritage in art, music, child-rearing activities, and values to gain strength to cope with slavery and develop a strong culture in an unfamiliar land?

15. Describe the variety of measures used to resist or avoid slavery and discuss their effectiveness.

16. Explain the causes, course, and consequences of the Seven Years' War (French and Indian War) and the overhaul of English imperial policy following the Treaty of Paris in 1763.

17. What were the conflicting goals and perspectives of the Americans and British in the aftermath of the Seven Years' War (French and Indian War)?

CHAPTER 4
The Road to Independence

A NEW COLONIAL SYSTEM

The Revolution was effected before the war commenced. The Revolution was in the hearts and minds of the people.

—former President John Adams, 1818

Although some believe that the history of the American Revolution began long before the first shots were fired in 1775, England and America did not begin an overt parting of the ways until 1763, more than a century and a half after the founding of the first permanent settlement at Jamestown, Virginia. The colonies had grown vastly in economic strength and cultural attainment, and virtually all had long years of self-government behind them. In the 1760s, their combined population exceeded 1,500,000—a sixfold increase since 1700.

In the aftermath of the French and Indian War, Britain needed a new imperial design, but the situation in America was anything but favorable to change. Long accustomed to a large measure of independence, the colonies were demanding more—not less—freedom, particularly now that the French menace had been eliminated. To put a new system into effect and to tighten control, Parliament had to contend with colonists trained in self-government and impatient with interference.

One of the first things that the British attempted was the organization of the interior. The conquest of Canada and of the Ohio Valley necessitated policies that would not alienate the French and Indian inhabitants. But here the Crown came into conflict with the interests of the colonies. Fast increasing in population, and needing more land for settlement, various colonies claimed the right to extend their boundaries as far west as the Mississippi River.

The British government, fearing that settlers migrating into the new lands would provoke a series of Indian wars, believed that the lands should be opened to colonists on a more gradual basis. Restricting movement was also a way of ensuring royal control over existing settlements before allowing the formation of new ones. The Royal Proclamation of 1763 reserved all the western territory between the Alleghenies, Florida, the Mississippi River, and Quebec for use by Native Americans. Thus the Crown attempted to sweep away every western land claim of the thirteen colonies and to stop westward expansion. Though never effectively enforced, this measure, in the eyes of the colonists, constituted a high-handed disregard of their most elementary right to occupy and settle western lands.

More serious in its repercussions was the new financial policy of the British government, which needed more money to support its growing empire. Unless the taxpayer in England was to supply all money for the colonies' defense, revenues would have to be extracted from the colonists through a stronger central administration, which would come at the expense of colonial self-government.

The first step in inaugurating the new system was the replacement of the Molasses Act of 1733, which placed a prohibitive duty, or tax, on the import of rum and molasses from non-English areas, with the Sugar Act of 1764. This act forbade the importation of foreign rum; put a modest duty on molasses from all sources; and levied duties on wines, silks, coffee, and a number of other luxury items. The hope was that lowering the duty on molasses would reduce the temptation to smuggle it from the Dutch and French West Indies for processing in the rum distilleries of New England. To enforce the Sugar Act, customs officials were ordered to show more energy and effectiveness. British warships in American waters were instructed to seize smugglers, and "writs of assistance," or warrants, authorized the king's officers to search suspected premises.

Both the duty imposed by the Sugar Act and the measures to enforce it caused consternation among New England merchants. They contended that payment of even the small duty imposed would be ruinous to their businesses. Merchants, legislatures, and town meetings protested the law, and colonial lawyers found in the preamble of the Sugar Act the first intimation of "taxation without representation," the slogan that was to draw many to the American cause against the mother country.

Later in 1764, Parliament enacted a Currency Act "to prevent paper bills of credit hereafter issued in any of his Majesty's colonies from being made legal tender." Since the colonies were a deficit trade area and were constantly short of hard currency, this measure added a serious burden to the colonial economy. Equally objectionable from the colonial viewpoint was the Quartering Act, passed in 1765, which required colonies to provide royal troops with provisions and barracks.

1. The Royal Proclamation of 1763 reserved the area between the Alleghenies and the Mississippi to

   a. American colonists.
   b. French colonists.
   c. English settlers.
   d. Native Americans.

2. The colonists thought that the Royal Proclamation of 1763 was

   a. fair.
   b. just.
   c. reasonable.
   d. high-handed and violating their rights.

3. The duty on molasses imported from English areas was increased by

   a. the Molasses Act of 1733.
   b. the Sugar Act of 1764.
   c. the Currency Act of 1764.
   d. the Quarterly Act of 1765.

4. New England merchants were particularly upset by the passage and enforcement of

   a. the Molasses Act of 1733.
   b. the Sugar Act of 1764.
   c. the Currency Act of 1764.
   d. the Quarterly Act of 1765.

43

STAMP ACT

The last of the measures inaugurating the new colonial system sparked the greatest organized resistance. Known as the "Stamp Act," it provided that revenue stamps be affixed to all newspapers, broadsides, pamphlets, licenses, leases, or other legal documents, the revenue (collected by American customs agents) to be used for "defending, protecting and securing" the colonies.

The Stamp Act bore equally on people who did any kind of business. Thus it aroused the hostility of the most powerful and articulate groups in the American population: journalists, lawyers, clergymen, merchants, and businessmen, north and south, east and west. Soon leading merchants organized for resistance and formed non-importation associations.

Trade with the mother country fell off sharply in the summer of 1765, as prominent men organized themselves into the "Sons of Liberty"—secret organizations formed to protest the Stamp Act, often through violent means. From Massachusetts to South Carolina, the act was nullified, and mobs, forcing luckless customs agents to resign their offices, destroyed the hated stamps.

Spurred by delegate Patrick Henry, the Virginia House of Burgesses passed a set of resolutions in May denouncing taxation without representation as a threat to colonial liberties. The House of Burgesses declared that Virginians had the rights of Englishmen, and hence could be taxed only by their own representatives. On June 8, the Massachusetts Assembly invited all the colonies to appoint delegates to the so-called Stamp Act Congress in New York, held in October 1765, to consider appeals for relief from the king and Parliament. Twenty-seven representatives from nine colonies seized the opportunity to mobilize colonial opinion against parliamentary interference in American affairs. After much debate, the congress adopted a set of resolutions asserting that "no taxes ever have been or can be constitutionally imposed on them, but by their respective legislatures," and that the Stamp Act had a "manifest tendency to subvert the rights and liberties of the colonists."

1. The Stamp Act required revenue stamps to be purchased and affixed to all

   a. residences.
   b. places of business.
   c. publications and legal documents.
   d. weapons.

2. The Stamp Act did **not** offend

   a. farmers.
   b. journalists, lawyers, and clergymen.
   c. merchants and businessmen.
   d. the southern colonies.

3. Reaction to the Stamp Act did **not** involve
   a. avoiding imports.
   b. ceasing trade among the colonies.
   c. violent protests.
   d. pressure on customs agents.

44

4. The secret organizations formed in 1765 to protest the Stamp Act were called

   a. the Virginia House of Burgesses.
   b. the Massachusetts Assembly.
   c. Stamp Act Congress.
   d. Sons of Liberty.

TAXATION WITHOUT REPRESENTATION

The issue thus drawn centered on the question of representation. From the colonies' point of view, it was impossible to consider themselves represented in Parliament unless they actually elected members to the House of Commons. But this idea conflicted with the English principle of "virtual representation," according to which each member of Parliament represented the interests of the whole country, even the empire, despite the fact that his electoral base consisted of only a tiny minority of property owners from a given district. The rest of the community was seen to be "represented" on the ground that all inhabitants shared the same interests as the property owners who elected members of Parliament.

Most British officials held that Parliament was an imperial body representing and exercising the same authority over the colonies as over the homeland. The American leaders argued that no "imperial" Parliament existed; their only legal relations were with the Crown. It was the king who had agreed to establish colonies beyond the sea and the king who provided them with governments. They argued that the king was equally a king of England and a king of the colonies, but they insisted that the English Parliament had no more right to pass laws for the colonies than any colonial legislature had the right to pass laws for England.

The British Parliament was unwilling to accept the colonial contentions. British merchants, however, feeling the effects of the American boycott, threw their weight behind a repeal movement, and in 1766 Parliament yielded, repealing the Stamp Act and modifying the Sugar Act. However, to mollify the supporters of central control over the colonies, Parliament followed these actions with the passage of the Declaratory Act. This act asserted the authority of Parliament to make laws binding the colonies "in all cases whatsoever."

1. The American leaders felt their only legal relationship was with

   a. the House of Commons.
   b. Parliament.
   c. their virtual representatives in Parliament.
   d. the Crown.

2. The Stamp Act was repealed and the Sugar Act modified in 1766 because of pressure from

   a. Parliament.
   b. British merchants.
   c. the Stamp Act Congress.
   d. the Crown.

3. After repeal of the Stamp Act, Parliament

    a. asserted its absolute authority over the colonies.
    b. ceded authority to colonial legislatures.
    c. ceded authority to the king.
    d. asserted authority over town matters only.

TOWNSHEND ACTS

The year 1767 brought another series of measures that stirred anew all the elements of discord. Charles Townshend, British chancellor of the exchequer, was called upon to draft a new fiscal program. Intent upon reducing British taxes by making more efficient the collection of duties levied on American trade, he tightened customs administration, at the same time sponsoring duties on colonial imports of paper, glass, lead, and tea exported from Britain to the colonies. The so-called Townshend Acts were based on the premise that taxes imposed on goods imported by the colonies were legal, while internal taxes (like the Stamp Act) were not.

The Townshend Acts were designed to raise revenue to be used in part to support colonial governors, judges, customs officers, and the British army in America. In response, Philadelphia lawyer John Dickinson, in *Letters of a Pennsylvania Farmer*, argued that Parliament had the right to control imperial commerce, but did not have the right to tax the colonies, whether the duties were external or internal.

The agitation following enactment of the Townshend duties was less violent than that stirred by the Stamp Act, but it was nevertheless strong, particularly in the cities of the eastern seaboard. Merchants once again resorted to non-importation agreements, and people made do with local products. Colonists, for example, dressed in homespun clothing and found substitutes for tea. They used homemade paper and their houses went unpainted. In Boston, enforcement of the new regulations provoked violence. When customs officials sought to collect duties, they were set upon by the populace and roughly handled. For this infraction, two British regiments were dispatched to protect the customs commissioners.

The presence of British troops in Boston was a standing invitation to disorder. On March 5, 1770, antagonism between citizens and British soldiers again flared into violence. What began as a harmless snowballing of British soldiers degenerated into a mob attack. Someone gave the order to fire. When the smoke had cleared, three Bostonians lay dead in the snow. Dubbed the "Boston Massacre," the incident was dramatically pictured as proof of British heartlessness and tyranny.

Faced with such opposition, Parliament in 1770 opted for a strategic retreat and repealed all the Townshend duties except that on tea, which was a luxury item in the colonies, imbibed only by a very small minority. To most, the action of Parliament signified that the colonists had won a major concession, and the campaign against England was largely dropped. A colonial embargo on "English tea" continued, but was not too scrupulously observed. Prosperity was increasing and most colonial leaders were willing to let the future take care of itself.

1. The Townshend Acts taxed American

    a. internal trade.
    b. products.
    c. custom administration.
    d. imports.

2. The Townshend Acts were **not** designed to pay for

   a. colonial governors.
   b. British troops in America.
   c. The King's personal expenses.
   d. Colonial judges and customs officials.

3. John Dickinson said that parliament had no right to collect taxes on either colonial internal or external trade in his

   a. *Letters of a Philadelphia Lawyer.*
   b. *Letters of a Pennsylvania Farmer.*
   c. *Letters of a Philadelphia Farmer.*
   d. *Letters of a Pennsylvania Lawyer.*

4. The reaction of the colonist to the Townshend Acts included all of the following **except**

   a. painting their houses red, white, and blue.
   b. using homespun clothing.
   c. using homemade paper.
   d. giving up tea.

5. In Boston, the reaction to the collection of the Townshend Acts duties was particularly violent, so the British government

   a. withdrew two British regiments from Boston.
   b. stationed two British regiments in Boston.
   c. withdrew the customs commissioners.
   d. assigned more customs commissioners.

6. Resentment of the British troops led to colonists

   a. shooting three British soldiers.
   b. insulting three British soldiers.
   c. attacking a group of British soldiers with snowballs.
   d. attacking a group of British soldiers with guns.

7. When British troops fired on the mob attacking them on March 5, 1770, resulting in three deaths, it became known as

   a. a symbol of mob violence.
   b. the Townshend Act.
   c. the Boston Tea Party.
   d. the Boston Massacre.

8. Parliament backed off, repealing all Townshend duties **except** the one on

   a. coffee.
   b. tea.
   c. rum
   d. molasses

SAMUEL ADAMS AND THE BOSTON "TEA PARTY"

During a three-year interval of calm, a relatively small number of radicals strove energetically to keep the controversy alive, however. They contended that payment of the tax constituted an acceptance of the principle that Parliament had the right to rule over the colonies. They feared that at any time in the future, the principle of parliamentary rule might be applied with devastating effect on all colonial liberties.

The radicals' most effective leader was Samuel Adams of Massachusetts, who toiled tirelessly for a single end: independence. From the time he graduated from Harvard College in 1740, Adams was a public servant in some capacity—inspector of chimneys, tax-collector, and moderator of town meetings. A consistent failure in business, he was shrewd and able in politics, with the New England town meeting his theater of action.

Adams's goals were to free people from their awe of social and political superiors, make them aware of their own power and importance and thus arouse them to action. Toward these objectives, he published articles in newspapers and made speeches in town meetings, instigating resolutions that appealed to the colonists' democratic impulses.

In 1772, he induced the Boston town meeting to select a "Committee of Correspondence" to state the rights and grievances of the colonists. The committee opposed a British decision to pay the salaries of judges from customs revenues; it feared that the judges would no longer be dependent on the legislature for their incomes and thus no longer accountable to it, thereby leading to the emergence of "a despotic form of government." The committee communicated with other towns on this matter and requested them to draft replies. Committees were set up in virtually all the colonies, and out of them grew a base of effective revolutionary organizations. Still, Adams did not have enough fuel to set a fire.

In 1773, however, Britain furnished Adams and his allies with an incendiary issue. The powerful East India Company, finding itself in critical financial straits, appealed to the British government, which granted it a monopoly on all tea exported to the colonies. The government also permitted the East India Company to supply retailers directly, bypassing colonial wholesalers who had previously sold it. After 1770, such a flourishing illegal trade existed that most of the tea consumed in America was of foreign origin and imported, illegally, duty-free. By selling its tea through its own agents at a price well under the customary one, the East India Company made smuggling unprofitable and threatened to eliminate the independent colonial merchants at the same time. Aroused not only by the loss of the tea trade but also by the monopolistic practice involved, colonial traders joined the radicals agitating for independence.

In ports up and down the Atlantic coast, agents of the East India Company were forced to resign, and new shipments of tea were either returned to England or warehoused. In Boston, however, the agents defied the colonists and, with the support of the royal governor, made preparations to land incoming cargoes regardless of opposition. On the night of December 16, 1773, a band of men disguised as Mohawk Indians and led by Samuel Adams boarded three British ships lying at anchor and dumped their tea cargo into Boston harbor. They took this step because they feared that if the tea were landed, colonists would actually comply with the tax and purchase the tea. Adams and his band of radicals doubted their countrymen's commitment to principle.

A crisis now confronted Britain. The East India Company had carried out a parliamentary statute, and if the destruction of the tea went unpunished, Parliament would admit to the world that it had no control over the colonies. Official opinion in Britain almost unanimously condemned the Boston Tea Party as an act of vandalism and advocated legal measures to bring the insurgent colonists into line.

48

1. After the repeal of most of the Townshend Acts duties,

    a. most Americans continued agitating against Parliament.
    b. only Samuel Adams and a few radicals continued agitating against Parliament.
    c. prosperity across America included Samuel Adams's business.
    d. even Samuel Adams stopped agitating for democracy.

2. In 1772, Samuel Adams induced Boston to organize the first of many

    a. Committees of Correspondence.
    b. Tea Parties.
    c. town meetings.
    d. movements to make judges independent of legislatures.

3. After 1770, most tea imported to America

    a. came from England.
    b. was grown domestically.
    c. was subject to duty.
    d. came from non-English sources and was illegal and duty-free.

4. In 1773, the British government

    a. declared the East India Company bankrupt.
    d. required the East India Company to sell tea only to wholesalers.
    c. gave the East India Company a tea monopoly and allowed it to sell directly.
    d. allowed the East India Company to charge a must higher price for tea.

5. Colonial traders objected to the fact that, with the East India Company selling tea directly,

    a. tea would be cheaper.
    b. tea would be more expensive.
    c. tea would be taxed.
    c. tea would be tax free.

6. Radicals objected to the fact that, with the East India Company selling tea directly,

    a. tea would be cheaper.
    b. tea would be more expensive.
    c. tea would be taxed.
    c. tea would be tax free.

7. The East India Company gave in to protest at most ports, but planned to force the issue in

    a. Philadelphia.
    b. Boston.
    c. Charleston.
    d. New York.

8. On December 16, 1773 the Boston Tea Party occurred because

    a. Mohawk Indians did not like tea.
    b. Samuel Adams knew colonists would not drink the tea.
    c. Samuel Adams did not like tea.
    d. Samuel Adams was afraid the colonists would acquiesce to British taxes.

THE COERCIVE ACTS

Parliament responded with new laws that the colonists called the "Coercive or Intolerable Acts." The first, the Boston Port Bill, closed the port of Boston until the tea was paid for, an action that threatened the very life of the city, for to prevent Boston from having access to the sea meant economic disaster. Other enactments restricted local authority and banned most town meetings held without the governor's consent. A Quartering Act required local authorities to find suitable quarters for British troops, in private homes if necessary. Instead of subduing and isolating Massachusetts as Parliament intended, these acts rallied its sister colonies to its aid.

The Quebec Act, passed at nearly the same time, extended the boundaries of the province of Quebec and guaranteed the right of the French inhabitants to enjoy religious freedom and their own legal customs. The colonists opposed this act because, by disregarding old charter claims to western lands, it threatened to hem them in to the North and Northwest by a Roman Catholic–dominated province. Though the Quebec Act had not been passed as a punitive measure, it was classed by the Americans with the Coercive Acts, and all became known as the "Five Intolerable Acts."

At the suggestion of the Virginia House of Burgesses, colonial representatives met in Philadelphia on September 5, 1774, "to consult upon the present unhappy state of the Colonies." Delegates to this meeting, known as the First Continental Congress, were chosen by provincial congresses or popular conventions. Every colony except Georgia sent at least one delegate, and the total number of fifty-five was large enough for diversity of opinion, but small enough for genuine debate and effective action. The division of opinion in the colonies posed a genuine dilemma for the delegates. They would have to give an appearance of firm unanimity to induce the British government to make concessions and, at the same time, they would have to avoid any show of radicalism or spirit of independence that would alarm more moderate Americans. A cautious keynote speech, followed by a "resolve" that no obedience was due the Coercive Acts, ended with adoption of a set of resolutions, among them the right of the colonists to "life, liberty and property," and the right of provincial legislatures to set "all cases of taxation and internal polity."

The most important action taken by the Congress, however, was the formation of a "Continental Association," which provided for the renewal of the trade boycott and for a system of committees to inspect customs entries, publish the names of merchants who violated the agreements, confiscate their imports, and encourage frugality, economy, and industry.

The Association immediately assumed the leadership in the colonies, spurring new local organizations to end what remained of royal authority. Led by the pro-independence leaders, they drew their support not only from the less well-to-do, but from many members of the professional class, especially lawyers, most of the planters of the southern colonies, and a number of merchants. They intimidated the hesitant into joining the popular movement and punished the hostile. They began the collection of military supplies and the mobilization of troops. And they fanned public opinion into revolutionary ardor.

Many Americans, opposed to British encroachment on American rights, nonetheless favored discussion and compromise as the proper solution. This group included Crown-appointed officers, many Quakers and members of other religious sects opposed to the use of violence, many merchants—especially from the middle colonies—and some discontented farmers and frontiersmen from southern colonies.

The king might well have effected an alliance with these large numbers of moderates and, by timely concessions, so strengthened their position that the revolutionaries would have found it difficult to

50

proceed with hostilities. But George III had no intention of making concessions. In September 1774, scorning a petition by Philadelphia Quakers, he wrote, "The die is now cast, the Colonies must either submit or triumph." This action isolated the Loyalists who were appalled and frightened by the course of events following the Coercive Acts.

1. The Coercive or Intolerable Acts were in response to

    a. the Committees of Correspondence.
    b. the Townshend Acts.
    c. the Boston Massacre.
    d. the Boston Tea Party.

2. Which of the following was **not** one of the Intolerable Acts?

    a. the Boston Port Bill
    b. the Stamp Act
    c. the Quartering Act
    d. the Quebec Act

3. In response to the Intolerable Acts, colonial representatives did **not**

    a. meet in Philadelphia.
    b. make concessions to the British government.
    c. condemn the Coercive Acts.
    d. assert the colonists' right to life, liberty, and property.

4. The first Continental Congress meeting in 1774 formed a Continental Association that did all of the following **except**

    a. encourage open debate and differing points of view.
    b. assume leadership in the colonies.
    c. unite the less well-to-do with lawyers, planters, and merchants.
    d. collect military supplies and fan revolutionary spirit.

5. Prominent among moderates were all of the following **except**

    a. Quakers and others opposed to violence.
    b. merchants from the middle colonies.
    c. New England lawyers.
    d. Loyalists with strong ties to England.

6. George III

    a. encouraged the moderates.
    b. worked to resolve differences.
    c. offered concessions.
    d. took a hard line.

THE REVOLUTION BEGINS

General Thomas Gage, an amiable English gentleman with an American-born wife, commanded the garrison at Boston, where political activity had almost wholly replaced trade. Gage's main duty in the colonies had been to enforce the Coercive Acts. When news reached him that the Massachusetts colonists were collecting powder and military stores at the town of Concord, thirty-two kilometers away, Gage sent a strong detail from the garrison to confiscate these munitions.

After a night of marching, the British troops reached the village of Lexington on April 19, 1775, and saw a grim band of seventy Minutemen—so named because they were said to be ready to fight in a minute—through the early morning mist. The Minutemen intended only a silent protest, but Major John Pitcairn, the leader of the British troops, yelled, "Disperse, you damned rebels! You dogs, run!" The leader of the Minutemen, Captain John Parker, told his troops not to fire unless fired at first. The Americans were withdrawing when someone fired a shot, which led the British troops to fire at the Minutemen. The British then charged with bayonets, leaving eight dead and ten wounded. It was, in the often quoted phrase of Ralph Waldo Emerson, "the shot heard 'round the world."

Then the British pushed on to Concord. The Americans had taken away most of the munitions, but the British destroyed whatever was left. In the meantime, American forces in the countryside mobilized, moved toward Concord, and inflicted casualties on the British, who began the long return to Boston. All along the road, however, behind stone walls, hillocks, and houses, militiamen from "every Middlesex village and farm" made targets of the bright red coats of the British soldiers. By the time the weary soldiers stumbled into Boston, they suffered more than two hundred and fifty killed and wounded. The Americans lost ninety-three men.

While the alarms of Lexington and Concord were still resounding, the Second Continental Congress met in Philadelphia, Pennsylvania, on May 10, 1775. By May 15th, the Congress voted to go to war, inducting the colonial militias into continental service and appointing Colonel George Washington of Virginia as commander-in-chief of the American forces. In the meantime, the Americans would suffer high casualties at Bunker Hill just outside Boston. Congress also ordered American expeditions to march northward into Canada by fall. Although the Americans later captured Montreal, they failed in a winter assault on Quebec and eventually retreated to New York.

Despite the outbreak of armed conflict, the idea of complete separation from England was still repugnant to some members of the Continental Congress. In July, John Dickinson had drafted a resolution, known as the "Olive Branch Petition," begging the king to prevent further hostile actions until some sort of agreement could be worked out. The petition fell on deaf ears, however, and King George III issued a proclamation on August 23, 1775, declaring the colonies to be in a state of rebellion.

Britain had expected the southern colonies to remain loyal, in part because of their reliance on slavery. Many in the southern colonies feared that a rebellion against the mother country would also trigger a slave uprising against the planters. In November 1775, in fact, Lord Dunmore, the governor of Virginia, offered freedom to all slaves who would fight for the British. However, Dunmore's proclamation had the effect of driving to the rebel side many Virginians who would otherwise have remained Loyalist.

The governor of North Carolina, Josiah Martin, also urged North Carolinians to remain loyal to the Crown. When one thousand five hundred men answered Martin's call, they were defeated by revolutionary armies before British troops could arrive to help.

52

British warships continued down the coast to Charleston, South Carolina, and opened fire on the city in early June 1776. But South Carolinians had time to prepare, and repulsed the British by the end of the month. They would not return south for more than two years.

1. General Gage sent troops to Concord to

   a. collect duties.
   b. suppress trade.
   c. confiscate munitions.
   d. take prisoners.

2. The Minutemen in Lexington

   a. fired first under orders from Captain John Parker.
   b. began to withdraw.
   c. refused to withdraw.
   d. charged the British with bayonets.

3. The shot heard 'round the world, on April 19, 1775, the first shot of the revolution, was fired in Lexington by

   a. Major John Pitcairn.
   b. the British.
   c. the Americans.
   d. nobody knows who.

4. After leaving Lexington, the British

   a. never reached Concord.
   b. reached Concord without a fight.
   c. confiscated all the American munitions.
   d. retreated directly to Boston.

5. During the retreat to Boston,

   a. the British killed or wounded 250 Americans.
   b. the British lost 93 men.
   c. the Americans killed or wounded 250 British.
   d. the British hid behind stone walls.

6. Before the Continental Congress could convene in Philadelphia,

   a. George Washington was named commander-in-chief.
   b. the colonial militias were inducted into continental service.
   c. Congress voted to go to war.
   d. the Americans suffered heavy casualties at Bunker Hill.

7. Congress ordered an attack on

   a. Boston.
   b. Charleston.
   c. Canada.
   d. Florida.

8. The attack succeeded at Montreal, but failed at _____, and ended in retreat.

   a. Quebec
   b. Nova Scotia
   c. South Carolina
   d. North Carolina

9. John Dickinson, author of *Letters of a Pennsylvania Farmer*, was the leader of

   a. the attack on Canada.
   b. efforts to retain ties with England.
   c. a proclamation that the colonies were in rebellion.
   d. a move to free the slaves of Virginia.

10. In general, the southern states were expected by England to

   a. free the slaves.
   b. remain loyal to England.
   c. accept occupation of Charleston.
   d. led the revolution.

COMMON SENSE AND INDEPENDENCE

In January 1776, Thomas Paine, a political theorist and writer who had come to America from England in 1774, published a fifty-page pamphlet, "Common Sense." Within three months, 100,000 copies of the pamphlet were sold. Paine attacked the idea of hereditary monarchy, declaring that one honest man was worth more to society than "all the crowned ruffians that ever lived." He presented the alternatives—continued submission to a tyrannical king and an outworn government, or liberty and happiness as a self-sufficient, independent republic. Circulated throughout the colonies, "Common Sense" helped to crystallize the desire for separation.

There still remained the task, however, of gaining each colony's approval of a formal declaration. On May 10, 1776—one year to the day since the Second Continental Congress had first met—a resolution was adopted calling for separation. Now only a formal declaration was needed. On June 7th, Richard Henry Lee of Virginia introduced a resolution declaring, "That these United Colonies are, and of right ought to be, free and independent states. . . . " Immediately, a committee of five, headed by Thomas Jefferson of Virginia, was appointed to prepare a formal declaration.

Largely Jefferson's work, the Declaration of Independence, adopted on July 4, 1776, not only announced the birth of a new nation, but also set forth a philosophy of human freedom that would become a dynamic force throughout the entire world. The Declaration draws upon French and English Enlightenment political philosophy, but one influence in particular stands out: John Locke's *Second Treatise on Government*. Locke took conceptions of the traditional rights of Englishmen and universalized them into the natural rights of all humankind. The Declaration's familiar opening passage echoes Locke's social-contract theory of government:

> We hold these truths to be self-evident, that all men are created equal, that they are endowed by their Creator with certain unalienable Rights, that among these are Life, Liberty and the pursuit of Happiness. That to secure these rights, Governments are instituted among Men, deriving their just powers from the consent of the governed, that whenever any Form of Government becomes destructive of these ends, it is the Right of the People to alter or to abolish it, and to institute a new Government, laying its foundation on such principles, and organizing its powers in such form, as to them shall seem most likely to effect their Safety and Happiness.

In the Declaration, Jefferson linked Locke's principles directly to the situation in the colonies. To fight for American independence was to fight for a government based on popular consent in place of a government by a king who had "combined with others to subject us to a jurisdiction foreign to our constitution, and unacknowledged by our laws. . . . " Only a government based on popular consent could secure natural rights to life, liberty, and the pursuit of happiness. Thus, to fight for American independence was to fight on behalf of one's own natural rights.

1. The one document that helped more than any other rally support among Americans for independence was

    a. John Dickinson's "Olive Branch Petition," July 1775.
    b. Richard Henry Lee's resolution, June 7, 1776.
    c. Thomas Paine's "Common Sense" pamphlet, January 1776.
    d. Thomas Jefferson's Declaration of Independence, July 4, 1776.

2. The Declaration of Independence was based on theories of natural rights of humankind and social contract government found in

    a. Benjamin Franklin's Albany Plan of Union.
    b. John Dickinson's *Letter of a Pennsylvania Farmer*.
    c. John Locke's **Second Treatise on Government**.
    d. Thomas Paine's "Common Sense."

3. Jefferson stated that governments

    a. do not require the consent of the governed.
    b. are not instituted to secure the rights of men.
    c. can be abolished if they do not protect rights.
    d. cannot be altered or abolished.

4. Jefferson argued that the fight for independence was a fight

    a. for natural rights.
    b. for freedom from taxation without representation.
    c. against a government based on popular consent.
    d. for the right to vote.

DEFEATS AND VICTORIES

Although the Americans suffered severe setbacks for months after independence was declared, their tenacity and perseverance eventually paid off. During August 1776, in the Battle of Long Island in New York, Washington's position became untenable, and he executed a masterly retreat in small boats from Brooklyn to the Manhattan shore. British General William Howe twice hesitated and allowed the Americans to escape. By November, however, Howe had captured Fort Washington on Manhattan Island. New York City would remain under British control until the end of the war.

By December, Washington's forces were nearing collapse, as supplies and promised aid failed to materialize. But Howe again missed his chance to crush the Americans by deciding to wait until spring to resume fighting. In the meantime, Washington crossed the Delaware River, north of Trenton, New Jersey. In the early morning hours of December 26th, his troops surprised the garrison at Trenton, taking more than nine hundred prisoners. A week later, on January 3, 1777, Washington attacked the British at Princeton, regaining most of the territory formally occupied by the British. The victories at Trenton and Princeton revived flagging American spirits.

In 1777, Howe defeated the American army at Brandywine in Pennsylvania and occupied Philadelphia, forcing the Continental Congress to flee. Washington had to endure the bitterly cold winter of 1777–1778 at Valley Forge, Pennsylvania, lacking adequate food, clothing, and supplies. The American troops suffered less because of shortages of these items than because farmers and merchants preferred exchanging their goods for British gold and silver rather than for paper money issued by the Continental Congress and the states.

Valley Forge was the lowest ebb for Washington's Continental Army, but 1777 proved to be the turning point in the war. In late 1776, British General John Burgoyne devised a plan to invade New York and New England via Lake Champlain and the Hudson River. Unfortunately, he had too much heavy equipment to negotiate the wooded and marshy terrain. At Oriskany, New York, a band of Loyalists and Indians under Burgoyne's command ran into a mobile and seasoned American force. At Bennington, Vermont, more of Burgoyne's forces, seeking much-needed supplies, encountered American troops. The ensuing battle delayed Burgoyne's army long enough to enable Washington to send reinforcements from the lower Hudson River near Albany, New York. By the time Burgoyne resumed his advance, the Americans were waiting for him. Led by Benedict Arnold—who would later betray the Americans at West Point, New York—the Americans twice repulsed the British. Burgoyne fell back to Saratoga, New York, where American forces under General Horatio Gates surrounded the British troops. On October 17, 1777, Burgoyne surrendered his entire army. The British lost six generals, three hundred other officers, and five thousand five hundred enlisted personnel.

1. Washington revived Americas hopes with victory in

   a. the Battle of Long Island, August 1776.
   b. the fight for Fort Washington, November 1776.
   c. the fight to control Manhattan, November 1776.
   d. the Battles of Trenton and Princeton, New Jersey, December 1776 and January 1777.

2. After the loss of Manhattan, the Americans also

   a. lost Philadelphia after the Battle of Brandywine.
   b. lost at Valley Forge, Pennsylvania.
   c. lost at Oriskany, New York.
   d. lost at Bennington, Vermont.

56

3. The turning point of the war was

   a. Benedict Arnold's betrayal at West Point.
   b. Burgoyne's advance down the Hudson River.
   c. Burgoyne's defeat and surrender at Saratoga, October 1777.
   d. General Horatio Gates's defeat at Saratoga.

FRANCO-AMERICAN ALLIANCE

In France, enthusiasm for the American cause was high: the French intellectual world was itself in revolt against feudalism and privilege. However, the Crown lent its support to the colonies for geopolitical rather than ideological reasons; the French government had been eager for reprisal against Britain ever since France's defeat in 1763. To further the American cause, Benjamin Franklin was sent to Paris in 1776. His wit, guile, and intellect soon made their presence felt in the French capital and played a major role in winning French assistance.

France began providing aid to the colonies in May 1776, when it sent fourteen ships with war supplies to America. In fact, most of the gunpowder used by the American armies came from France. After Britain's defeat at Saratoga, France saw an opportunity to seriously weaken its ancient enemy and restore the balance of power that had been upset by the Seven Years' War (the French and Indian War). On February 6, 1778, America and France signed a Treaty of Amity and Commerce, in which France recognized America and offered trade concessions. They also signed a Treaty of Alliance, which stipulated that if France entered the war, neither country would lay down its arms until America won its independence, that neither would conclude peace with Britain without the consent of the other, and that each guaranteed the other's possessions in America. This was the only bilateral defense treaty signed by the United States or its predecessors until 1949.

The Franco-American alliance soon broadened the conflict. In June 1778, British ships fired on French vessels and the two countries went to war. In 1779, Spain, hoping to reacquire territories taken by Britain in the Seven Years' War, entered the conflict on the side of France, but not as an ally of the Americans. In 1780, Britain declared war on the Dutch, who had continued to trade with the Americans. The combination of these European powers, with France in the lead, was a far greater threat to Britain than the American colonies standing alone.

1. The French supported the Americans mainly because

   a. they believed in freedom.
   b. they believed in equality.
   c. they believed in liberty.
   d. they wanted to get back at the British.

2. Even before Saratoga, the French had provided the Americans with supplies and gunpowder largely because of the influence of

   a. the Dutch.
   b. the Spanish.
   c. John Adams.
   d. Benjamin Franklin.

3. After Saratoga, the French signed an alliance with the Americans in 1778 and

    a. France and England went to war.
    b. Spain declared war on France.
    c. France declared war on the Dutch.
    d. the Seven Years' War commenced.

THE BRITISH MOVE SOUTH—VICTORY AND INDEPENDENCE

With the French now involved, the British stepped up their efforts in the southern colonies since they felt that most southerners were Loyalists. A campaign began in late 1778, with the capture of Savannah, Georgia. Shortly thereafter, British troops drove toward Charleston, South Carolina, the principal southern port. The British also brought naval and amphibious forces into play there, and they managed to bottle up American forces on the Charleston peninsula. On May 12th, General Benjamin Lincoln surrendered the city and its five thousand troops, the greatest American defeat of the war.

But the reversal in fortune only emboldened the American rebels. Soon, South Carolinians began roaming the countryside, attacking British supply lines. By July, American General Horatio Gates, who had assembled a replacement force of untrained militiamen, rushed to Camden, South Carolina, to confront British forces led by General Charles Cornwallis. But the untrained soldiers of Gates's army panicked and ran when confronted by the British regulars. Cornwallis's troops met the Americans several more times, but the most significant battle took place at Cowpens, South Carolina, in early 1781, where the Americans soundly defeated the British. After an exhausting but unproductive chase through North Carolina, Cornwallis set his sights on Virginia.

In July 1780, France's Louis XVI had sent to America an expeditionary force of six thousand men under the Comte Jean de Rochambeau. In addition, the French fleet harassed British shipping and prevented reinforcement and resupply of British forces in Virginia by a British fleet sailing from New York City. French and American armies and navies, totaling eighteen thousand men, parried with Cornwallis all through the summer and into the fall. Finally, on October 19, 1781, after being trapped at Yorktown near the mouth of Chesapeake Bay, Cornwallis surrendered his army of eight thousand British soldiers.

Although Cornwallis's defeat did not immediately end the war—which would drag on inconclusively for almost two more years—a new British government decided to pursue peace negotiations in Paris in early 1782, with the American side represented by Benjamin Franklin, John Adams, and John Jay. On April 15, 1783, Congress approved the final treaty, and Great Britain and its former colonies signed it on September 3rd. Known as the Treaty of Paris, the peace settlement acknowledged the independence, freedom, and sovereignty of the thirteen former colonies—now states—to which Great Britain granted the territory west to the Mississippi River, north to Canada, and south to Florida, which was returned to Spain. The fledgling colonies that Richard Henry Lee had spoken of more than seven years before had finally become "free and independent states." The task of knitting together a nation yet remained.

1. The British decided to fight in the American South because

    a. they already controlled most of the North.
    b. they thought that most southerners were Loyalists.
    c. the weather was better.
    d. their supply lines were shorter.

58

2. The Americans suffered their worst defeat of the war at

   a. Savannah, Georgia.
   b. Charleston, South Carolina.
   c. Camden, South Carolina.
   d. Cowpens, South Carolina.

3. The leader of the British forces in the South was General

   a. Frances Marion.
   b. Horatio Gates.
   c. Charles Cornwallis.
   d. Benjamin Lincoln.

4. The British were soundly defeated at

   a. Savannah, Georgia.
   b. Charleston, South Carolina.
   c. Camden, South Carolina.
   d. Cowpens, South Carolina.

5. The French fleet helped trap Cornwallis at _____ where he surrendered on October 19, 1781.

   a. New York City
   b. North Carolina
   c. Yorktown, Virginia
   d. Cowpens, South Carolina

6. In 1782, all of the following negotiated the Treaty of Paris, signed in 1783, **except**

   a. Comte Jean de Rochambeau.
   b. Benjamin Franklin.
   c. John Adams.
   d. John Jay.

7. Florida, which the British had taken possession of, was returned to

   a. the United States.
   b. France.
   c. Holland.
   d. Spain.

LOYALISTS DURING THE AMERICAN REVOLUTION

Americans today think of the War for Independence as a revolution, but in important respects it was also a civil war. American Loyalists, or "Tories" as their opponents called them, opposed the revolution, and many took up arms against the rebels. Estimates of the number of Loyalists range as high as 500,000, or twenty percent of the white population of the colonies.

What motivated the Loyalists? Most educated Americans, whether Loyalist or Revolutionary, accepted John Locke's theory of natural rights and limited government. Thus, the Loyalists, like the rebels, criticized such British actions as the Stamp Act and the Coercive Acts. Loyalists wanted to pursue peaceful forms of protest because they believed that violence would give rise to mob rule or tyranny. They also believed that independence would mean the loss of economic benefits derived from membership in the British mercantile system.

Loyalists came from all walks of life. The majority were small farmers, artisans, and shopkeepers. Not surprisingly, most British officials remained loyal to the Crown. Wealthy merchants tended to remain loyal, as did Anglican ministers, especially in Puritan New England. Loyalists also included some blacks (to whom the British promised freedom), Indians, indentured servants, and some German immigrants, who supported the Crown mainly because George III was of German origin.

The number of Loyalists in each colony varied. Recent estimates suggest that half the population of New York was Loyalist; it had an aristocratic culture and was occupied throughout the Revolution by the British. In the Carolinas, backcountry farmers were Loyalist, whereas the Tidewater planters tended to support the Revolution.

During the Revolution, most Loyalists suffered little from their views. However, a minority, about nineteen thousand Loyalists, armed and supplied by the British, fought in the conflict.

The Paris Peace Treaty required Congress to restore property confiscated from Loyalists. The heirs of William Penn in Pennsylvania, for example, and those of George Calvert in Maryland received generous settlements. In the Carolinas, where enmity between rebels and Loyalists was especially strong, few of the latter regained their property. In New York and the Carolinas, the confiscations from Loyalists resulted in something of a social revolution as large estates were parceled out to yeoman farmers.

About 100,000 Loyalists left the country, including William Franklin, the son of Benjamin, and John Singleton Copley, the greatest American painter of the period. Most settled in Canada. Some eventually returned, although several state governments excluded the Loyalists from holding public office. In the decades after the Revolution, Americans preferred to forget about the Loyalists. Apart from Copley, the Loyalists became nonpersons in American history.

1. American Revolutionaries were also called Whigs. Loyalists were also called

   a. a very small minority.
   b. over 40% of the white population.
   c. over 50% of the white population.
   d. Tories.

2. Loyalists

    a. rejected John Locke's arguments.
    b. were a very small minority of Americans.
    c. did not fight against their fellow Americans.
    d. worried about the loss of economic benefits.

3. Loyalists did **not**

    a. take up arms against their fellow Americans.
    b. include farmers, artisans, and shopkeepers.
    c. include most Tidewater planters.
    d. include many New Yorkers.

4. Loyalists

    a. lost most of their property in Pennsylvania.
    b. lost most of their property in the Carolinas.
    c. kept most of their property in New York.
    d. lost most of their property in Maryland.

5. One of the most prominent Loyalists, son of a royal prominent American Revolutionary, was _____, royal governor of New Jersey.

    a. William Franklin
    b. John Singleton Copley
    c. William Penn
    d. George Calvert

Chapter 4
Questions for Further Research

1. Describe the causes of the American Revolution, the ideas and interests involved, and the reasons for the American victory.

2. Describe the institutions and practices of government created during the revolution and how they were revised between 1787 and 1815 to create the foundation of the American political system.

3. Why did the English Parliament feel it was justified in taxing the colonies, and why and how did the colonists challenge the legitimacy of the new taxes?

4. Describe the chronology of the critical events leading to the outbreak of armed conflict between the American colonies and England.

5. Compare the effects of political and religious ideas and economic interests in bringing about revolution.

6. Explain the divisions in the colonies over taxation by comparing the interests and positions of Loyalists and Patriots from different economic groups.

7. Was the outbreak of conflict at Lexington and Concord almost inevitable? Why or why not?

8. Could either party after Lexington and Concord have prevented war? How?

9. What were the historical antecedents of the Declaration of Independence?

10. Explain the major ideas expressed in the Declaration of Independence and their sources.

11. What are the fundamental contradictions between the ideals expressed in the Declaration of Independence and the realities of chattel slavery?

12. Why was Jefferson chosen to write the Declaration of Independence?

13. What were the consequences of the Declaration of Independence? Analyze the character and roles of the military, political, and diplomatic leaders who helped forge the American victory.

14. Describe the chronology of the course of the war as it moved from the North in 1775–1778 to the South in 1778–1781, climaxing at Yorktown.

15. Analyze the major campaigns in the Revolutionary War and assess the leadership of both American and British military leaders.

16. Analyze the varied responses of Native American nations to the American Revolution using the Iroquois and Cherokee as case studies.

17. Why did both the British and Americans seek alliances with Indian nations?

18. What were Mohawk chief Joseph Brant's reasons for supporting Britain after the Oswego Council (1777)?

19. Why did free blacks and slaves join the Patriots during the war? Were their expectations met?

20. Describe the comparative advantages and disadvantages of such efforts to finance the Revolutionary War as taxing Americans, borrowing from foreign nations, confiscating goods and requiring services needed by the military, printing unbacked paper money, and repudiating debts.

21. Compare and contrast the interests, goals, and actions of France, Holland, and Spain in responding to American requests for assistance in their war with England.

22. Analyze the terms of the Treaty of Paris, and their implications for U.S. relationships with Native Americans and with the European powers that continued to hold territories and interests in North America.

23. Could the underfinanced and undermanned Americans have defeated the most powerful military force in the Western world without French aid?

24. What might have happened if the French army and navy had not been available to assist Washington at Yorktown?

25. Assess the contributions to the American victory of individual Europeans.

26. How did white land hunger affect relations with Native Americans after the Treaty of Paris?

CHAPTER 5
The Formation of a National Government

STATE CONSTITUTIONS

The success of the Revolution gave Americans the opportunity to give legal form to their ideals as expressed in the Declaration of Independence, and to remedy some of their grievances through state constitutions. As early as May 10, 1776, Congress had passed a resolution advising the colonies to form new governments "such as shall best conduce to the happiness and safety of their constituents." Some of them had already done so, and within a year after the Declaration of Independence, all but three had drawn up constitutions.

The new constitutions showed the impact of democratic ideas. None made any drastic break with the past, since all were built on the solid foundation of colonial experience and English practice. But each was also animated by the spirit of republicanism, an ideal that had long been praised by Enlightenment philosophers.

Naturally, the first objective of the framers of the state constitutions was to secure those "unalienable rights" whose violation had caused the former colonies to repudiate their connection with Britain. Thus, each constitution began with a declaration or bill of rights. Virginia's, which served as a model for all the others, included a declaration of principles, such as popular sovereignty, rotation in office, freedom of elections, and an enumeration of fundamental liberties: moderate bail and humane punishment, speedy trial by jury, freedom of the press and of conscience, and the right of the majority to reform or alter the government.

Other states enlarged the list of liberties to guarantee freedom of speech, of assembly, and of petition, and frequently included such provisions as the right to bear arms, to the writ of *habeas corpus*, to inviolability of domicile, and to equal protection under the law. Moreover, all the constitutions paid allegiance to the three-branch structure of government—executive, legislative, and judiciary—each checked and balanced by the others.

Pennsylvania's constitution was the most radical. In that state, Philadelphia artisans, Scots-Irish frontiersmen, and German-speaking farmers had taken control. The provincial congress adopted a constitution that permitted every male taxpayer and his sons to vote, required rotation in office (no one could serve as a representative more than four years out of every seven), and set up a single-chamber legislature.

The state constitutions had some glaring limitations, particularly by more recent standards. Constitutions established to guarantee people their natural rights did not secure for everyone the most fundamental natural right—equality. The colonies south of Pennsylvania excluded their slave populations from their inalienable rights as human beings. Women had no political rights. No state went so far as to permit universal male suffrage, and even in those states that permitted all taxpayers to vote (Delaware, North Carolina, and Georgia, plus Pennsylvania), office-holders were required to own a certain amount of property.

1. The state constitution of _____ served as a model for the others.

    a. Virginia
    b. Pennsylvania
    c. North Carolina
    d. Georgia

2. All constitutions

    a. allowed slaves to vote.
    b. allowed all taxpayers to vote.
    c. established checks and balances.
    d. guaranteed freedom of speech, assembly, and petition.

3. The most radical constitution was that of

    a. Virginia.
    b. Pennsylvania.
    c. North Carolina.
    d. Georgia.

4. _____ did **not** permit all taxpayers to vote.

    a. Delaware
    b. North Carolina
    c. Georgia
    d. Virginia

5. _____ permitted adult male children of taxpayers to vote.

    a. Virginia
    b. Pennsylvania
    c. North Carolina
    d. Georgia

6. Women could **not** vote in

    a. some states.
    b. many states.
    c. most states.
    d. all states.

64

7. Pennsylvania's constitution was supported by all of the following groups **except**
    a. Quakers.
    b. Philadelphia artisans.
    c. Scots-Irish frontiersmen.
    d. German-speaking farmers.

ARTICLES OF CONFEDERATION

The struggle with England had done much to change colonial attitudes. Local assemblies had rejected the Albany Plan of Union in 1754, refusing to surrender even the smallest part of their autonomy to any other body, even one they themselves had elected. However, in the course of the Revolution, mutual aid had proved effective and the fear of relinquishing individual authority had lessened to a large degree.

John Dickinson produced the "Articles of Confederation and Perpetual Union" in 1776. The Continental Congress adopted them in November 1777, and they went into effect in 1781, having been ratified by all the states. The governmental framework established by the Articles had many weaknesses. The national government lacked the authority to set up tariffs when necessary, to regulate commerce, and to levy taxes. It lacked sole control of international relations; a number of states had begun their own negotiations with foreign countries. Nine states had organized their own armies and several had their own navies. There was a curious hodgepodge of coins and a bewildering variety of state and national paper bills, all quickly depreciating in value.

Economic difficulties after the war prompted calls for change. The end of the war had a severe effect on merchants who supplied the armies of both sides and who had lost the advantages deriving from participation in the British mercantile system. The states gave preference to American goods in their tariff policies, but these tariffs were inconsistent, leading to the demand for a stronger central government to implement a uniform policy.

Farmers probably suffered the most from economic difficulties following the Revolution. The supply of farm produce exceeded demand, and unrest centered chiefly among farmer-debtors who wanted strong remedies to avoid foreclosure on their property and imprisonment for debt. Courts were clogged with suits for debt. All through the summer of 1786, popular conventions and informal gatherings in several states demanded reform in the state administrations.

In the autumn of 1786, mobs of farmers in Massachusetts under the leadership of a former army captain, Daniel Shays, began forcibly to prevent the county courts from sitting and passing further judgments for debt, pending the next state election. In January 1787, a ragtag army of one thousand two hundred farmers moved toward the federal arsenal at Springfield. The rebels, armed chiefly with staves and pitchforks, were repulsed by a small state militia force. General Benjamin Lincoln then arrived with reinforcements from Boston and routed the remaining Shays sites, whose leader escaped to Vermont. The government captured fourteen rebels and sentenced them to death, but ultimately pardoned some and let the others off with short prison terms. After the defeat of the rebellion, a newly-elected legislature, whose majority sympathized with the rebels, met some of their demands for debt relief.

1. The author of the Articles of Confederation was _____, who had also written *Letters of a Pennsylvania Farmer*, asserting American rights, and the Olive Branch Petition, seeking to avoid a complete break with England.

    a. Samuel Adams
    b. John Adams
    c. John Dickinson
    d. Benjamin Franklin

2. The Articles of Confederation went into effect in 1781,

    a. during the French and Indian War.
    b. before the American Revolution.
    c. during the American Revolution.
    d. after the Treaty of Paris ended the Revolution.

3. The Articles of Confederation provided for a national government that

    a. had the power to set tariffs.
    b. had the power to regulate commerce.
    c. had the power to levy taxes.
    d. lacked the power to levy taxes or tariffs.

4. Under the Articles of Confederation, the national government

    a. had sole control of international relations.
    b. did not have sole control of international relations.
    c. had the sole authority to organize an army and navy.
    d. had the sole authority to issue money.

5. By 1786, merchants and _____ facing economic difficulties and under heavy burdens of debt sought reform.

    a. bankers
    b. lawyers
    c. farmers
    d. legislators

6. In Massachusetts, the aim of Daniel Shays's rebellion of 1786–1787 was to

    a. stop courts from enforcing debts.
    b. disband state militias.
    c. force federal troops out of Massachusetts.
    d. allow farmers to escape to Vermont.

7. Massachusetts elected a new government that

    a. executed fourteen rebels.
    b. deported Daniel Shays to Vermont.
    c. deported Benjamin Franklin to Vermont.
    d. passed some reforms and debt relief.

66

THE PROBLEM OF EXPANSION

With the end of the Revolution, the United States again had to face the old unsolved Western question—the problem of expansion, with its complications of land, fur trade, Indians, settlement, and local government. Lured by the richest land yet found in the country, pioneers poured over the Appalachian Mountains and beyond. By 1775, the far-flung outposts scattered along the waterways had tens of thousands of settlers. Separated by mountain ranges and hundreds of kilometers from the centers of political authority in the East, the inhabitants established their own governments. Settlers from all the tidewater states pressed on into the fertile river valleys, hardwood forests, and rolling prairies of the interior. By 1790, the population of the trans-Appalachian region numbered well over 120,000.

Before the war, several colonies had laid extensive and often overlapping claims to land beyond the Appalachians. To those without such claims, this rich territorial prize seemed unfairly apportioned. Maryland, speaking for the latter group, introduced a resolution that the western lands be considered common property to be parceled by the Congress into free and independent governments. This idea was not received enthusiastically. Nonetheless, in 1780, New York led the way by ceding its claims to the United States. In 1784, Virginia, which held the grandest claims, relinquished all land north of the Ohio River. Other states ceded their claims. It became apparent that Congress would come into possession of all the lands north of the Ohio River and west of the Allegheny Mountains. This common possession of millions of acres was the most tangible evidence yet of nationality and unity, and gave a certain substance to the idea of national sovereignty. At the same time, these vast territories were a problem that required solution.

The Articles of Confederation offered an answer. Under the Articles, a system of limited self-government (set forth in the Northwest Ordinance of 1787) provided for the organization of the Northwest Territory, initially as a single district, ruled by a governor and judges appointed by the Congress. When this territory had five thousand free male inhabitants of voting age, it was to be entitled to a legislature of two chambers, itself electing the lower house. In addition, it could at that time send a non-voting delegate to Congress.

No more than five nor fewer than three states were to be formed out of this territory. Whenever any one of them had sixty thousand free inhabitants, it was to be admitted to the Union "on an equal footing with the original states in all respects." The Ordinance guaranteed civil rights and liberties, encouraged education, and guaranteed that "there shall be neither slavery nor involuntary servitude in the said territory."

The new policy repudiated the time-honored concept that colonies existed for the benefit of the mother country and were politically subordinate and socially inferior. That doctrine was replaced by the principle that colonies are but the extension of the nation and are entitled, not as a privilege but as a right, to all the benefits of equality. These enlightened provisions of the Northwest Ordinance formed the basis for America's public land policy.

1. Settlers from Tidewater states were attracted over the Appalachians by all of the following **except**

   a. fertile river valleys.
   b. hardwood forests.
   c. rolling prairies.
   d. peaceful, friendly relations with the Indians.

67

2. The population of the trans-Appalachian region exceeded 120,000 by

   a. 1775.
   b. 1780.
   c. 1784.
   d. 1790.

3. Most states ceded their rights to the trans-Appalachian lands and land north of the Ohio River in the

   a. 1760s.
   b. 1770s.
   c. 1780s.
   d. 1790s.

4. The first state to cede its rights was

   a. Maryland.
   b. New York.
   c. Virginia.
   d. Connecticut.

5. Possession of millions of acres of land by _____ offered proof of national sovereignty.

   a. New York
   b. Virginia
   c. the United States
   d. the Northwest Ordinance

6. The _____ guaranteed rights of limited self-government, admission to the Union, and civil rights and liberties in the Northwest Territory.

   a. Albany Plan of Union
   b. Articles of Confederation
   c. Shays Rebellion
   d. Northwest Ordinance of 1787

CONSTITUTIONAL CONVENTION

George Washington wrote of the period between the Treaty of Paris and the writing of the Constitution that the states were united only by a "rope of sand." Disputes between Maryland and Virginia over navigation on the Potomac River led to a conference of representatives of five states at Annapolis, Maryland, in 1786. One of the delegates, Alexander Hamilton, convinced his colleagues that commerce was too much bound up with other political and economic questions, and that the situation was too serious to be dealt with by so unrepresentative a body.

He advocated calling upon all the states to appoint representatives for a meeting to be held the following spring in Philadelphia. The Continental Congress was at first indignant over this bold step, but its protests were cut short by the news that Virginia had elected George Washington a delegate. During the next fall and winter, elections were held in all states but Rhode Island.

It was a gathering of notables that assembled at the Federal Convention in the Philadelphia State House in May 1787. The state legislatures sent leaders with experience in colonial and state governments, in Congress, on the bench, and in the army. George Washington, regarded as the country's outstanding citizen because of his integrity and his military leadership during the Revolution, was chosen as presiding officer.

Prominent among the more active members were two Pennsylvanians: Gouverneur Morris, who clearly saw the need for national government, and James Wilson, who labored indefatigably for the national idea. Also elected by Pennsylvania was Benjamin Franklin, nearing the end of an extraordinary career of public service and scientific achievement. From Virginia came James Madison, a practical young statesman, a thorough student of politics and history, and, according to a colleague, "from a spirit of industry and application . . . the best-informed man on any point in debate." Madison today is recognized as the "Father of the Constitution."

Massachusetts sent Rufus King and Eldridge Gerry, young men of ability and experience. Roger Sherman, shoemaker-turned-judge, was one of the representatives from Connecticut. From New York came Alexander Hamilton, who had proposed the meeting. Absent from the Convention were Thomas Jefferson, who was serving in France as minister, and John Adams, serving in the same capacity in Great Britain. Youth predominated among the fifty-five delegates—the average age was forty-two.

The Convention had been authorized merely to draft amendments to the Articles of Confederation, but as Madison later wrote, the delegates, "with a manly confidence in their country," simply threw the Articles aside and went ahead with the building of a wholly new form of government.

They recognized that the paramount need was to reconcile two different powers—the power of local control, which was already being exercised by the thirteen semi-independent states, and the power of a central government. They adopted the principle that the functions and powers of the national government, being new, general, and inclusive, had to be carefully defined and stated, while all other functions and powers were to be understood as belonging to the states. But realizing that the central government had to have real power, the delegates also generally accepted the fact that the government should be authorized—among other things—to coin money, to regulate commerce, to declare war, and to make peace.

1. The impetus for a Constitutional Convention was

    a. George Washington calling unity a "rope of sand."
    b. disputes between Virginia and Maryland over navigation on the Potomac.
    c. Rhode Island's failure to elect delegates.
    d. the Treaty of Paris.

2. The idea for a Constitutional Convention came from

    a. George Washington.
    b. Benjamin Franklin.
    c. Alexander Hamilton.
    d. James Madison.

3. The debate for or against a convention ended with news that _____ had been elected a delegate.

    a. George Washington
    b. Benjamin Franklin
    c. Alexander Hamilton
    d. James Madison

4. _____ was chosen presiding officer of the Convention.

   a. George Washington
   b. Benjamin Franklin
   c. Alexander Hamilton
   d. James Madison

5. Representatives from Pennsylvania did **not** include

   a. Gouverneur Morris.
   b. James Wilson.
   c. Benjamin Franklin.
   d. Roger Sherman.

6. The Convention was supposed to

   a. elect a President.
   b. write a new Constitution.
   c. draft amendments to the Articles of Confederation.
   d. resolve the dispute between Maryland and Virginia.

7. _____ was not at the Convention because he was serving as minister to France.

   a. Rufus King
   b. Eldridge Gerry
   c. John Adams
   d. Thomas Jefferson

8. _____ was not at the Convention because he was serving as minister to England.

   a. Rufus King
   b. Eldridge Gerry
   c. John Adams
   d. Thomas Jefferson

DEBATE AND COMPROMISE

The 18th-century statesmen who met in Philadelphia were adherents of Montesquieu's concept of the balance of power in politics. This principle was supported by colonial experience and strengthened by the writings of John Locke, with which most of the delegates were familiar. These influences led to the conviction that three equal and coordinate branches of government should be established. Legislative, executive, and judicial powers were to be so harmoniously balanced that no one could ever gain control. The delegates agreed that the legislative branch, like the colonial legislatures and the British Parliament, should consist of two houses.

On these points there was unanimity within the assembly. But sharp differences arose as to the method of achieving them. Representatives of the small states—New Jersey, for instance—objected to changes that would reduce their influence in the national government by basing representation upon population rather than upon statehood, as was the case under the Articles of Confederation.

On the other hand, representatives of large states, like Virginia, argued for proportionate representation. This debate threatened to go on endlessly until Roger Sherman came forward with arguments for representation in proportion to the population of the states in one house of Congress, the House of Representatives, and equal representation in the other, the Senate.

The alignment of large against small states then dissolved. But almost every succeeding question raised new problems, to be resolved only by new compromises. Northerners wanted slaves counted when determining each state's tax share, but not in determining the number of seats a state would have in the House of Representatives. According to a compromise reached with little dissent, the House of Representatives would be apportioned according to the number of free inhabitants plus three-fifths of the slaves.

Certain members, such as Sherman and Eldridge Gerry, still smarting from the Shays Rebellion, feared that the mass of people lacked sufficient wisdom to govern themselves and thus wished no branch of the federal government to be elected directly by the people. Others thought the national government should be given as broad a popular base as possible. Some delegates wished to exclude the growing West from the opportunity of statehood; others championed the equality principle established in the Northwest Ordinance of 1787.

There was no serious difference on such national economic questions as paper money, laws concerning contract obligations, or the role of women, who were excluded from politics. But there was a need for balancing sectional economic interests; for settling arguments as to the powers, term, and selection of the chief executive; and for solving problems involving the tenure of judges and the kind of courts to be established.

Laboring through a hot Philadelphia summer, the Convention finally achieved a draft incorporating in a brief document the organization of the most complex government yet devised—a government supreme within a clearly defined and limited sphere. In conferring powers, the Convention gave the federal government full power to levy taxes, borrow money, establish uniform duties and excise taxes, coin money, fix weights and measures, grant patents and copyrights, set up post offices, and build post roads. The national government also had the power to raise and maintain an army and navy, and to regulate interstate commerce. It was given the management of Indian affairs, foreign policy, and war. It could pass laws for naturalizing foreigners and controlling public lands, and it could admit new states on the basis of absolute equality with the old. The power to pass all necessary and proper laws for executing these clearly defined powers rendered the federal government able to meet the needs of later generations and of a greatly expanded body politic.

The principle of separation of powers had already been given a fair trial in most state constitutions and had proved sound. Accordingly, the Convention set up a governmental system with separate legislative, executive, and judiciary branches—each checked by the others. Thus congressional enactments were not to become law until approved by the president. And the president was to submit the most important of his appointments and all his treaties to the Senate for confirmation. The president, in turn, could be impeached and removed by Congress. The judiciary was to hear all cases arising under federal laws and the Constitution; in effect, the courts were empowered to interpret both the fundamental and the statute law. But members of the judiciary, appointed by the president and confirmed by the Senate, could also be impeached by Congress.

To protect the Constitution from hasty alteration, Article V stipulated that amendments to the Constitution be proposed either by two-thirds of both houses of Congress or by two-thirds of the states meeting in convention. The proposals were to be ratified by one of two methods: either by the legislatures of three-fourths of the states, or by convention in three-fourths of the states, with the Congress proposing the method to be used.

Finally, the Convention faced the most important problem of all: how should the powers given to the new government be enforced? Under the Articles of Confederation, the national government had possessed—on paper—significant powers, which, in practice, had come to naught, for the states paid no attention to them. What was to save the new government from the same fate?

At the outset, most delegates furnished a single answer—the use of force. But it was quickly seen that the application of force upon the states would destroy the Union. The decision was that the government should not act upon the states but upon the people within the states, and should legislate for and upon all the individual residents of the country. As the keystone of the Constitution, the Convention adopted two brief but highly significant statements:

> Congress shall have power . . . to make all laws which shall be necessary and proper for carrying into execution the . . . powers vested by this Constitution in the Government of the United States . . . (Article I, Section 7)

> This Constitution and the laws of the United States, which shall be made in pursuance thereof; and all treaties made, or which shall be made, under the authority of the United States, shall be the supreme law of the land; and the judges in every State shall be bounding. (Article VI)

Thus the laws of the United States became enforceable in its own national courts, through its own judges and marshals, as well as in the state courts through the state judges and state law officers.

Debate continues to this day about the motives of those who wrote the Constitution. In 1913, Charles Beard, in *An Economic Interpretation of the Constitution*, argued that the Founding Fathers stood to gain economic advantages from the stability imposed by a powerful and authoritative national government because they held large amounts of depreciated government securities. However, James Madison, principal drafter of the constitution, held no bonds, while some opponents of the Constitution held large amounts of bonds and securities. Economic interests influenced the course of the debate, but so did state, sectional, and ideological interests. Equally important was the idealism of the framers. Products of the Enlightenment, the Founding Fathers designed a government that, they believed, would promote individual liberty and public virtue. The ideals embodied in the U.S. Constitution are an essential element of the American national identity.

1. Everyone agreed with Montesquieu's concept of

    a. strong central government.
    b. majority rights.
    c. minority rights.
    d. balance of power.

2. Montesquieu's principles were echoed in the writings of _____, whose work most of the delegates knew well.

    a. John Milton
    b. John Locke
    c. Karl Marx
    d. Charles Dickens

3. Basing representation in the legislature purely on population, rather than equally state by state, was opposed by small states like

    a. New York.
    b. Pennsylvania.
    c. New Jersey.
    d. Virginia.

4. The "Connecticut Compromise," one house based on each principle, was suggested by

    a. Roger Sherman.
    b. Gouverneur Morris.
    c. George Washington.
    d. Benjamin Franklin.

5. An example of the checks and balances written into the Constitution is

    a. the federal government's right to levy taxes and borrow and coin money.
    b. the federal government's authority to raise an army and navy.
    c. the federal government's power to regulate commerce, foreign policy, and war.
    d. the requirement that Congressional Legislation normally required the approval of the President.

6. The Constitution and laws of the United States were made the supreme law of the land, binding on and enforceable in state courts as well as federal courts in _____ of the Constitution.

    a. Article I, Section 7
    b. Article V
    c. Article VI
    d. the Preamble

7. The decision to count each slave as three-fifths of a person for the House of Representative's purpose was

    a. wise.
    b. fair.
    c. a necessary, if irrational, compromise.
    d. logical.

8. The framers of the Constitution were motivated

    a. by a combination of sectional, ideological, and personal interests.
    b. primarily to protect their own economic interests.
    c. out of idealism.
    d. out of patriotism.

RATIFICATION AND THE BILL OF RIGHTS

On September 17, 1787, after sixteen weeks of deliberation, the finished Constitution was signed by thirty-nine of the forty-two delegates present. Franklin, pointing to the half-sun painted in brilliant gold on the back of Washington's chair, said, "I have often in the course of the session . . . looked at that [chair] behind the president, without being able to tell whether it was rising or setting; but now, at length, I have the happiness to know that it is a rising, and not a setting, sun."

The Convention was over; the members "adjourned to the City Tavern, dined together, and took a cordial leave of each other." Yet a crucial part of the struggle for a more perfect union was yet to be faced. The consent of popularly elected state conventions was still required before the document could become effective.

The Convention had decided that the Constitution would take effect upon ratification by conventions in nine of the thirteen states. By June 1788, the required nine states ratified the Constitution, but the large states of Virginia and New York had not. Most people felt that without the support of these two states, the Constitution would never be honored. To many, the document seemed full of dangers; would not the strong central government that it established tyrannize them, oppress them with heavy taxes, and drag them into wars?

Differing views on these questions brought into existence two parties, the Federalists, who favored a strong central government, and the Antifederalists, who preferred a loose association of separate states. Impassioned arguments on both sides were voiced by the press, the legislatures, and the state conventions.

In Virginia, the Antifederalists attacked the proposed new government by challenging the opening phrase of the Constitution: "We the People of the United States." Without using the individual state names in the Constitution, the delegates argued, the states would not retain their separate rights or powers. Virginia Antifederalists were led by Patrick Henry, who became the chief spokesman for backcountry farmers who feared the powers of the new central government. Wavering delegates were persuaded by a proposal that the Virginia convention recommend a bill of rights, and Antifederalists joined with the Federalists to ratify the Constitution on June 25th.

In New York, Alexander Hamilton, John Jay, and James Madison pushed for the ratification of the Constitution in a series of essays known as "The Federalist Papers." The essays, published in New York newspapers, provided a now-classic argument for a central federal government, with separate executive, legislative, and judicial branches that checked and balanced one another. With "The Federalist Papers" influencing the New York delegates, the Constitution was ratified on July 26th.

Antipathy toward a strong central government was only one concern among those opposed to the Constitution; of equal concern to many was the fear that the Constitution did not protect individual rights and freedoms sufficiently. Virginian George Mason, author of Virginia's 1776 Declaration of Rights, was one of three delegates to the Constitutional Convention who refused to sign the final document because it did not enumerate individual rights. Together with Patrick Henry, he campaigned vigorously against ratification of the Constitution by Virginia. Indeed, five states, including Massachusetts, ratified the Constitution on the condition that such amendments be added immediately.

When the first Congress convened in New York City in September 1789, the calls for amendments protecting individual rights were virtually unanimous. Congress quickly adopted twelve such amendments; by December 1791, enough states had ratified ten amendments to make them part of

74

the Constitution. Collectively, they are known as the Bill of Rights. Among their provisions: freedom of speech, press, religion, and the right to assemble peacefully, protest, and demand changes (First Amendment); protection against unreasonable searches, seizures of property, and arrest (Fourth Amendment); due process of law in all criminal cases (Fifth Amendment); right to a fair and speedy trial (Sixth Amendment); protection against cruel and unusual punishment (Eighth Amendment); and provision that the people retain additional rights not listed in the Constitution (Ninth Amendment).

Since the adoption of the Bill of Rights, only sixteen more amendments have been added to the Constitution. Although a number of the subsequent amendments revised the federal government's structure and operations, most followed the precedent established by the Bill of Rights and expanded individual rights and freedoms.

1. The question of whether or not to ratify the Constitution led to the formation of the

   a. Federalists, who opposed the Constitution.
   b. Antifederalists, who favored the Constitution.
   c. Federalists, who favored the Constitution.
   d. rising sun on the back of Washington's chair.

2. The Antifederalists, who feared too much power was given to the central government in the new Constitution, were led in Virginia by

   a. Patrick Henry.
   b. Alexander Hamilton.
   c. John Jay.
   d. James Madison.

3. Antifederalists in Virginia and Massachusetts were persuaded to ratify the Constitution only upon the promise of

   a. a change in the Preamble.
   b. an enumeration of the states.
   c. "The Federalist Papers."
   d. a bill of rights.

4. New York delegates voted to ratify the Constitution after being influenced by

   a. a change in the Preamble.
   b. an enumeration of the States.
   c. "The Federalist Papers."
   d. a bill of rights.

5. Joining Patrick Henry in opposition to the ratification of the Constitution in Virginia was the author of the 1776 Declaration of Rights,

   a. George Mason.
   b. Alexander Hamilton.
   c. John Jay.
   d. James Madison.

75

6. The Constitution was finally ratified in

   a. 1776.
   b. 1787.
   c. 1788.
   d. 1789.

7. The first Congress, convened in New York in 1789, adopted _____ amendments.

   a. 10
   b. 12
   c. 14
   d. 16

8. By December 1791, _____ amendments had been ratified.

   a. 10
   b. 12
   c. 14
   d. 16

9. The first ten amendments to the Constitution are known as

   a. freedom of speech.
   b. freedom of Religion.
   c. freedom of Press.
   d. the Bill of Rights.

10. Protection against unreasonable search and seizure is part of the _____ Amendment.

   a. First
   b. Fourth
   c. Fifth
   d. Sixth

11. Freedom of assembly is part of the _____ Amendment.

   a. First
   b. Fourth
   c. Fifth
   d. Sixth

12. Protection against cruel and unusual punishment is part of the _____ Amendment.

   a. Fourth
   b. Fifth
   c. Sixth
   d. Eighth

13. Due process of law in all criminal cases is part of the _____ Amendment.

   a. Fourth
   b. Fifth
   c. Sixth
   d. Eighth

14. The right to a fair and speedy trial is part of the _____ Amendment.

    a. Fourth
    b. Fifth
    c. Sixth
    d. Eighth

PRESIDENT WASHINGTON

One of the last acts of the Congress of the Confederation was to arrange for the first presidential election, setting March 4, 1789, as the date that the new government would come into being. One name was on everyone's lips for the new chief of state—George Washington—and he was unanimously chosen president on April 30, 1789. In words spoken by every president since, Washington pledged to execute the duties of the presidency faithfully and, to the best of his ability, to "preserve, protect and defend the Constitution of the United States."

When Washington took office, the new Constitution enjoyed neither tradition nor the full backing of organized public opinion. Moreover, the new government had to create its own machinery. No taxes were forthcoming. Until a judiciary could be established, laws could not be enforced. The army was small. The navy had ceased to exist.

Congress quickly created the Departments of State and Treasury, with Thomas Jefferson and Alexander Hamilton as their respective secretaries. Simultaneously, Congress established the federal judiciary, establishing not only a Supreme Court, with one chief justice and five associate justices, but also three circuit courts and thirteen district courts. Both a secretary of war and an attorney general were also appointed. And since Washington generally preferred to make decisions only after consulting those men whose judgment he valued, the American presidential Cabinet came into existence, consisting of the heads of all the departments that Congress might create.

Meanwhile, the country was growing steadily and immigration from Europe was increasing. Americans were moving westward: New Englanders and Pennsylvanians into Ohio; Virginians and Carolinians into Kentucky and Tennessee. Good farms were to be had for small sums; labor was in strong demand. The rich valley stretches of upper New York, Pennsylvania, and Virginia soon became great wheat-growing areas.

Although many items were still homemade, the Industrial Revolution was dawning in America. Massachusetts and Rhode Island were laying the foundation of important textile industries; Connecticut was beginning to turn out tinware and clocks; New York, New Jersey, and Pennsylvania were producing paper, glass, and iron. Shipping had grown to such an extent that on the seas the United States was second only to Britain. Even before 1790, American ships were traveling to China to sell furs and bring back tea, spices, and silk.

At this critical juncture in the country's growth, Washington's wise leadership was crucial. He organized a national government, developed policies for settlement of territories previously held by Britain and Spain, stabilized the northwestern frontier, and oversaw the admission of three new states: Vermont (1791), Kentucky (1792), and Tennessee (1796). Finally, in his farewell address, Washington warned the nation to "steer clear of permanent alliances with any portion of the foreign world." This advice influenced American attitudes toward the rest of the world for generations to come.

1. George Washington promised to "preserve, protect and defend the Constitution of the United States" in his

   a. inaugural address.
   b. State of the Union address.
   c. first press conference.
   d. farewell address.

2. Washington warned against entangling alliances in his

   a. inaugural address.
   b. State of the Union address.
   c. first press conference.
   d. farewell address.

3. Washington had to

   a. continue long-standing traditions.
   b. fight a new war with Great Britain.
   c. create a new government from whole cloth.
   d. protect a well-established governmental structure.

4. Thomas Jefferson was chosen the first

   a. Secretary of State.
   b. Secretary of Treasury.
   c. Secretary of War.
   d. Chief Justice.

5. Alexander Hamilton was chosen the first

   a. Secretary of State.
   b. Secretary of Treasury.
   c. Secretary of War.
   d. Chief Justice.

6. Settlers in Ohio came primarily from

   a. Virginia.
   b. North Carolina.
   c. South Carolina.
   d. New England and Pennsylvania.

7. Settlers from Virginia and the Carolinas tended to migrate into

   a. New England.
   b. New York.
   c. Florida.
   d Kentucky and Tennessee.

8. As agriculture expanded, the most important crop became

   a. wheat.
   b. tobacco.
   c. cotton.
   d. apples.

9. The textile industry began to grow in

    a. Connecticut.
    b. Massachusetts and Rhode Island.
    c. New York and New Jersey.
    d. Pennsylvania.

10. Tinware and clocks were the principal industrial products of

    a. Connecticut.
    b. Massachusetts and Rhode Island.
    c. New York and New Jersey.
    d. Pennsylvania.

11. During Washington's administration, whish of the following states was **not** admitted into the union?

    a. Vermont
    b. Kentucky
    c. Maine
    d. Tennessee

HAMILTON VS. JEFFERSON

The conflict that took shape in the 1790s between the Federalists and the Antifederalists exercised a profound impact on American history. The Federalists, led by Alexander Hamilton, who had married into the wealthy Schuyler family, represented the urban mercantile interests of the seaports; the Antifederalists, led by Thomas Jefferson, spoke for the rural and southern interests. The debate between the two concerned the power of the central government versus that of the states, with the Federalists favoring the former and the Antifederalists advocating states' rights.

Hamilton sought a strong central government acting in the interests of commerce and industry. He brought to public life a love of efficiency, order, and organization. In response to the call of the House of Representatives for a plan for the "adequate support of public credit," he laid down and supported principles not only of the public economy, but of effective government.

Hamilton pointed out that America must have credit for industrial development, commercial activity, and the operations of government. It must also have the complete faith and support of the people. There were many who wished to repudiate the national debt or pay only part of it. Hamilton, however, insisted upon full payment and also upon a plan by which the federal government took over the unpaid debts of the states incurred during the Revolution.

Hamilton also devised a Bank of the United States, with the right to establish branches in different parts of the country. He sponsored a national mint, and argued in favor of tariffs, using a version of an "infant industry" argument: that temporary protection of new firms can help foster the development of competitive national industries. These measures—placing the credit of the federal government on a firm foundation and giving it all the revenues it needed—encouraged commerce and industry, and created a solid phalanx of businessmen who stood firmly behind the national government.

Jefferson advocated a decentralized agrarian republic. He recognized the value of a strong central government in foreign relations, but he did not want it strong in other respects. Hamilton's great aim was more efficient organization, whereas Jefferson once said, "I am not a friend to a very energetic government." Hamilton feared anarchy and thought in terms of order; Jefferson feared tyranny and thought in terms of freedom.

The United States needed both influences. It was the country's good fortune that it had both men and could, in time, fuse and reconcile their philosophies. One clash between them, which occurred shortly after Jefferson took office as secretary of state, led to a new and profoundly important interpretation of the Constitution. When Hamilton introduced his bill to establish a national bank, Jefferson objected. Speaking for those who believed in states' rights, Jefferson argued that the Constitution expressly enumerates all the powers belonging to the federal government and reserves all other powers to the states. Nowhere was it empowered to set up a bank.

Hamilton contended that because of the mass of necessary detail, a vast body of powers had to be implied by general clauses, and one of these authorized Congress to "make all laws which shall be necessary and proper" for carrying out other powers specifically granted. The Constitution authorized the national government to levy and collect taxes, pay debts, and borrow money. A national bank would materially help in performing these functions efficiently. Congress, therefore, was entitled, under its implied powers, to create such a bank. Washington and the Congress accepted Hamilton's view—and an important precedent for an expansive interpretation of the federal government's authority.

1. The Federalists represented _____ interests.

    a. rural
    b. farming
    c. southern
    d. urban, mercantile

2. The Anti-Federalists favored

    a. urban interests.
    b. a strong central government.
    c. states' rights.
    d. Alexander Hamilton.

3. Hamilton did not support

    a. taking over the unpaid debts of states.
    b. a Bank of the United States.
    c. tariffs.
    d. states' rights.

4. Jefferson did not believe in

    a. an energetic government.
    b. a decentralized republic.
    c. powers being reserved to the state.
    d. limited power to the federal government.

5. _____ did not believe the federal government had implied powers beyond those expressly enumerated in the Constitution.

    a. Hamilton
    b. Washington
    c. Congress
    d. Jefferson

CITIZEN GENET AND FOREIGN POLICY

Although one of the first tasks of the new government was to strengthen the domestic economy and make the nation financially secure, the United States could not ignore foreign affairs. The cornerstones of Washington's foreign policy were to preserve peace, to give the country time to recover from its wounds, and to permit the slow work of national integration to continue. Events in Europe threatened these goals. Many Americans were watching the French Revolution with keen interest and sympathy, and in April 1793, news came that made this conflict an issue in American politics. France had declared war on Great Britain and Spain, and a new French envoy, Edmond Charles Genet—known as Citizen Genet—was coming to the United States.

After the execution of King Louis XVI in January 1793, Britain, Spain, and Holland had become involved in war with France. According to the Franco-American Treaty of Alliance of 1778, the United States and France were perpetual allies, and America was obliged to help France defend the West Indies. However, the United States, militarily and economically a very weak country, was in no position to become involved in another war with major European powers. On April 22, 1793, Washington effectively abrogated the terms of the 1778 treaty that made American independence possible by proclaiming the United States to be "friendly and impartial toward the belligerent powers." When Genet arrived, he was cheered by many citizens, but treated with cool formality by the government. Angered, he violated a promise not to outfit a captured British ship as a privateer. Genet then threatened to take his cause directly to the American people, over the head of the government. Shortly afterward, the United States requested his recall by the French government.

The Genet incident strained American relations with France at a time when relations with Great Britain were far from satisfactory. British troops still occupied forts in the West, property carried off by British soldiers during the Revolution had not been restored or paid for, and the British navy was seizing American ships bound for French ports. To settle these matters, Washington sent John Jay, first chief justice of the Supreme Court, to London as a special envoy, where he negotiated a treaty securing withdrawal of British soldiers from western forts and London's promise to pay damages for Britain's seizure of ships and cargoes in 1793 and 1794. Reflecting the weakness of the U.S. position, the treaty placed severe limitations on American trade with the West Indies and said nothing about either the seizure of American ships in the future, or "impressment"—the forcing of American sailors into British naval service. Jay also accepted the British view that naval stores and war materiel that were contraband could not be conveyed to enemy ports by neutral ships.

Jay's Treaty touched off a stormy disagreement over foreign policy between the Antifederalists, now called Republicans, and the Federalists. The Federalists favored a pro-British policy because the commercial interests they represented profited from trade with Britain. By contrast, the Republicans favored France, in large measure for ideological reasons, and regarded the Jay Treaty as too favorable to Britain. After long debate, however, the Senate ratified the treaty.

1. In 1793, France declared war on

    a. Germany.
    b. Russia.
    c. the United States.
    d. Britain and Spain.

2. The war was precipitated by

    a. the French Revolution and the execution of Louis XVI.
    b. Citizen Genet.
    c. an attack on the West Indies.
    d. Holland.

3. In order to win independence, the United States has agreed

    a. not to fight another war with Great Britain.
    b. not to invade the West Indies.
    c. to the Franco-American Treaty Alliance of 1778, making France and the U.S. perpetual allies.
    d. to support the French Revolution.

4. Faced with war between France and Britain, President George Washington

    a. rallied to the French cause.
    b. disavowed the treaty with France.
    c. lived up to his obligations.
    d. defended France's interest in the West Indies.

5. The French Ambassador to the U.S., Citizen Genet

    a. was received with great warmth by the government.
    b. was received with great respect by the government.
    c. was received coolly by the people of the U.S.
    d. was received coolly by the government.

6. Citizen Genet was _____ his promise not to outfit a privateer.

    a. happy with his reception and lived up to
    b. happy with his reception, but broke
    c. unhappy with his reception and broke
    d. unhappy with his reception, but lived up to

7. The United Stated asked for Citizen Genet to be recalled. This left relations

    a. good with France.
    b. good with Great Britain.
    c. bad with France, but good with Great Britain.
    d. bad with France and bad with Great Britain.

8. John Jay's treaty with Great Britain

    a. secured withdrawal of British troops from the West.
    b. opened up trade with the West Indies.
    c. banned "impressment."
    d. banned seizure of American ships in the future.

9. Jay's treaty was ratified despite

    a. the Antifederalists' (Republicans') support of Britain.
    b. the Federalists support of France.
    c. the Republicans support of France.
    d. the Federalists view that the treaty was too favorable for Britain.

ADAMS AND JEFFERSON

Washington retired in 1797, firmly declining to serve for more than eight years as the nation's head. His vice president, John Adams of Massachusetts, was elected the new president. Even before he entered the presidency, Adams had quarreled with Alexander Hamilton and thus was handicapped by a divided party.

These domestic difficulties were compounded by international complications; France, angered by Jay's recent treaty with Britain, used the British argument that food supplies, naval stores, and war material bound for enemy ports were subject to seizure by the French navy. By 1797, France had seized three hundred American ships and had broken off diplomatic relations with the United States. When Adams sent three other commissioners to Paris to negotiate, agents of Foreign Minister Charles Maurice de Talleyrand (whom Adams labeled X, Y, and Z in his report to Congress) informed the Americans that negotiations could only begin if the United States loaned France $12 million and bribed officials of the French government. American hostility to France rose to an excited pitch. The so-called XYZ Affair led to the enlistment of troops and the strengthening of the fledgling U.S. Navy.

In 1799, after a series of sea battles with the French, war seemed inevitable. In this crisis, Adams thrust aside the guidance of Hamilton, who wanted war, and sent three new commissioners to France. Napoleon, who had just come to power, received them cordially, and the danger of conflict subsided with the negotiation of the Convention of 1800, which formally released the United States from its 1778 defense alliance with France. However, reflecting American weakness, France refused to pay $20 million in compensation for American ships taken by the French navy.

Hostility to France led Congress to pass the Alien and Sedition Acts, which had severe repercussions for American civil liberties. The Naturalization Act, which changed the requirement for citizenship from five to 14 years, was targeted at Irish and French immigrants suspected of supporting the Republicans. The Alien Act, operative for two years only, gave the president the power to expel or imprison aliens in time of war. The Sedition Act proscribed writing, speaking, or publishing anything of "a false, scandalous and malicious" nature against the president or Congress. The few convictions won under the Sedition Act only created martyrs to the cause of civil liberties and aroused support for the Republicans.

The acts met with resistance. Jefferson and Madison sponsored the passage of the Kentucky and Virginia Resolutions by the legislatures of the two states in November and December 1798. According to the resolutions, states could "interpose" their views on federal actions and "nullify" them. The doctrine of nullification would be used later for the southern states' defense of their interests vis-a-vis the North on the question of the tariff, and, more ominously, slavery.

By 1800, the American people were ready for a change. Under Washington and Adams, the Federalists had established a strong government, but sometimes failing to honor the principle that the American government must be responsive to the will of the people, they had followed policies that alienated large groups. For example, in 1798, they had enacted a tax on houses, land, and slaves, affecting every property owner in the country.

Jefferson had steadily gathered behind him a great mass of small farmers, shopkeepers, and other workers, and they asserted themselves in the election of 1800. Jefferson enjoyed extraordinary favor because of his appeal to American idealism. In his inaugural address, the first such speech in the new capital of Washington, D.C., he promised "a wise and frugal government" to preserve order among the inhabitants, but would "leave them otherwise free to regulate their own pursuits of industry, and improvement."

Jefferson's mere presence in the White House encouraged democratic procedures. He taught his subordinates to regard themselves merely as trustees of the people. He encouraged agriculture and westward expansion. Believing America to be a haven for the oppressed, he urged a liberal naturalization law. By the end of his second term, his far-sighted secretary of the treasury, Albert Gallatin, had reduced the national debt to less than $560 million. As a wave of Jeffersonian fervor swept the nation, state after state abolished property qualifications for the ballot and passed more humane laws for debtors and criminals.

1. George Washington refused to run for a third term. He was succeeded by

    a. John Adams.
    b. Alexander Hamilton.
    c. Thomas Jefferson.
    d. John Jay.

2. France was angered by _____'s treaty with Great Britain.

    a. John Adams
    b. Alexander Hamilton
    c. Thomas Jefferson
    d. John Jay

3. By 1797, France has seized _____ American ships.

    a. 3
    b. 30
    c. 300
    d. 3000

4. The agents of Talleyrand who demanded a bribe before negotiating with the United States were labeled

    a. traitors.
    b. ABC.
    c. $12 million.
    d. XYZ.

84

5. In 1799, after the XYZ affair, seizure of ships, and sea battles, war with _____ seemed inevitable.

    a. Britain
    b. France
    c. Hamilton
    d. Jefferson

6. War tensions were relieved when _____ signed the Convention of 1800, which released the United States from the Treaty of 1778, but failed to compensate for seized ships.

    a. King George III
    b. King Louis XIV
    c. Talleyrand
    d. Napoleon

7. The Sedition Act, part of the Alien and Sedition acts, enacted out of hostility toward France,

    a. targeted Irish and French immigrants.
    b. changed the citizenship requirement to 14 years.
    c. severely limited freedoms of speech and press.
    d. gave the President the power to imprison aliens.

8. Jefferson and Madison encouraged Virginia and Kentucky to resist the Alien and Sedition Acts with what turned out to be the dangerous doctrine of

    a. review.
    b. nullification.
    c. appeal.
    d. resistance.

9. The Federalists' advocacy of a strong central government probably did not offend voters as much as their

    a. pro-French policies.
    b. idealism.
    c. property tax of 1798.
    d. responsiveness.

10. Thomas Jefferson was elected President in 1800 largely because voters were looking for

    a. more freedom and idealism.
    b. more stability.
    c. another Federalist presidency.
    d. pro-British policies.

11. With the presidency of Jefferson, state laws also became

    a. stricter.
    b. harsher.
    c. more restrictive.
    d. more democratic and humane.

LOUISIANA AND BRITAIN

One of Jefferson's acts doubled the area of the country. At the end of the Seven Years' War, France had ceded to Spain the territory west of the Mississippi River, with the port of New Orleans near its mouth—a port indispensable for the shipment of American products from the Ohio and Mississippi valleys. Shortly after Jefferson became president, Napoleon forced a weak Spanish government to cede the great tract called Louisiana back to France. The move filled Americans with apprehension and indignation. Napoleon's plans for a huge colonial empire just west of the United States threatened the trading rights and the safety of all American interior settlements. Jefferson asserted that if France took possession of Louisiana, "from that moment we must marry ourselves to the British fleet and nation."

Napoleon, knowing that another war with Great Britain was impending, resolved to fill his treasury and put Louisiana beyond the reach of the British by selling it to the United States. This put Jefferson in a constitutional quandary: the Constitution gave no office the power to purchase territory. At first, Jefferson wanted to amend the Constitution, but his advisers told him that delay might lead Napoleon to change his mind, and that the power to purchase territory was inherent in the power to make treaties. Jefferson relented, saying that "the good sense of our country will correct the evil of loose construction when it shall produce ill effects."

For $15 million, the United States obtained the "Louisiana Purchase" in 1803. It contained more than 828,000 square miles as well as the port of New Orleans. The nation had gained a sweep of rich plains, mountains, forests, and river systems that within eighty years would become the nation's heartland, and one of the world's great granaries.

As Jefferson began his second term in 1805, he declared American neutrality during the struggle between Great Britain and France. Although both sides sought to restrict neutral shipping to the other, British control of the seas made its interdiction and seizure much more serious than any actions by Napoleonic France.

By 1807, the British had built their navy to more than seven hundred warships manned by nearly 150,000 sailors and marines. The massive force controlled the sea lanes: blockading French ports, protecting British commerce, and maintaining the crucial links to Britain's colonies. Yet the men of the British fleet lived under such harsh conditions that it was impossible to obtain crews by free enlistment. Many sailors deserted and found refuge on U.S. vessels. In these circumstances, British officers regarded it as their right to search American ships and take off British subjects, to the great humiliation of the Americans. Moreover, British officers frequently impressed American seamen into their service.

When Jefferson issued a proclamation ordering British warships to leave U.S. territorial waters, the British reacted by impressing more sailors. Jefferson decided to rely on economic pressure to force the British to back down. In December 1807, Congress passed the Embargo Act, forbidding all foreign commerce. Ironically, the Republicans, the champions of limited government, had passed a law that vastly increased the powers of the national government. In a single year, American exports fell to one-fifth of their former volume. Shipping interests were almost ruined by the measure, and discontent rose in New England and New York. Agricultural interests found that they too were suffering heavily, for prices dropped drastically when the southern and western farmers could not export their surplus grain, cotton, meat, and tobacco.

The hope that the embargo would starve Great Britain into a change of policy failed. As the grumbling at home increased, Jefferson turned to a milder measure, which conciliated domestic shipping interests. In early 1809, he signed the Non-Intercourse Act permitting commerce with all countries except Britain or France and their dependencies.

James Madison succeeded Jefferson as president in 1809. Relations with Great Britain grew worse, and the two countries moved rapidly toward war. The president laid before Congress a detailed report, showing several thousand instances in which the British had impressed American citizens. In addition, northwestern settlers had suffered from attacks by Indians whom they believed had been incited by British agents in Canada. This led many Americans to favor conquest of Canada. Success in such an endeavor would eliminate British influence among the Indians and open up new lands for colonization. The desire to conquer Canada, coupled with deep resentment over impressment of sailors, generated war fervor, and the United States declared war on Britain in 1812.

1. After the Seven Years' War, France had ceded New Orleans and the land west of the Mississippi to

   a. Mexico.
   b. Spain.
   c. Great Britain.
   d. the United States.

2. Shortly after Thomas Jefferson became President, _____ forced the return of the area to France.

   a. Jefferson
   b. Great Britain
   c. Spain
   d. Napoleon

3. The French and Americans both wanted to

   a. fight the British.
   b. put Louisiana beyond the reach of the British.
   c. buy Louisiana.
   d. sell Louisiana.

4. Jefferson was concerned because

   a. Napoleon wanted to delay.
   b. he did not have $15 million.
   c. the Constitution did give power to purchase territory.
   d. he favored loose construction of the Constitution.

5. The British seized far more American ships and seamen than the French because

   a. the French had more ships.
   b. the French were more respectful of American rights.
   c. the French were more respectful of American power.
   d. the British had more ships.

6. In an effort to stop impressment, Jefferson and his fellow Republicans passed, in 1807, the
   _____ Act, banning all foreign commerce.

   a. Cargo
   b. Barge
   c. Embargo
   d. Non-Intercourse

7. The effects of the ban were severe, so in 1809 the _____ Act banned only trade with Britain and
   France.

   a. Cargo
   b. Barge
   c. Embargo
   d. Non-Intercourse

8. The United States declared war on Britain for all of the following reasons **except**

   a. a British attack on New Orleans.
   b. British impressment of thousands of sailors.
   c. possible British involvement in Indian attacks in the Northwest.
   d. a desire to conquer Canada.

WAR OF 1812

As the country prepared for yet another war with Britain, the United States suffered from internal divisions. While the South and West favored war, New York and New England opposed it because it interfered with their commerce. The declaration of war had been made with military preparations still far from complete. There were fewer than seven thousand regular soldiers, distributed in widely scattered posts along the coast, near the Canadian border, and in the remote interior. These soldiers were to be supported by the undisciplined militia of the states.

Hostilities between the two countries began with an invasion of Canada, which, if properly timed and executed, would have brought united action against Montreal. But the entire campaign miscarried and ended with the British occupation of Detroit. The U.S. Navy, however, scored successes and restored confidence. In addition, American privateers, swarming the Atlantic, captured five hundred British vessels during the fall and winter months of 1812 and 1813.

The campaign of 1813 centered on Lake Erie. General William Henry Harrison—who would later become president—led an army of militia, volunteers, and regulars from Kentucky with the object of reconquering Detroit. On September 12th, while he was still in upper Ohio, news reached him that Commodore Oliver Hazard Perry had annihilated the British fleet on Lake Erie. Harrison occupied Detroit and pushed into Canada, defeating the fleeing British and their Indian allies on the Thames River. The entire region now came under American control.

Another decisive turn in the war occurred a year later when Commodore Thomas Macdonough won a point-blank gun duel with a British flotilla on Lake Champlain in upper New York. Deprived of naval support, a British invasion force of ten thousand men retreated to Canada. At about the same time, the British fleet was harassing the eastern seaboard with orders to "destroy and lay waste." On the night of August 24, 1814, an expeditionary force burst into Washington, D.C., home of the federal government, and left it in flames. President James Madison fled to Virginia.

As the war continued, British and American negotiators each demanded concessions from the other. The British envoys decided to concede, however, when they learned of Macdonough's victory on Lake Champlain. Urged by the Duke of Wellington to reach a settlement, and faced with the depletion of the British treasury due in large part to the heavy costs of the Napoleonic Wars, the negotiators for Great Britain accepted the Treaty of Ghent in December 1814. It provided for the cessation of hostilities, the restoration of conquests, and a commission to settle boundary disputes. Unaware that a peace treaty had been signed, the two sides continued fighting in New Orleans, Louisiana. Led by General Andrew Jackson, the Americans scored the greatest land victory of the war.

While the British and Americans were negotiating a settlement, Federalist delegates selected by the legislatures of Massachusetts, Rhode Island, Connecticut, Vermont, and New Hampshire gathered in Hartford, Connecticut, in a meeting that symbolized opposition to "Mr. Madison's war." New England had managed to trade with the enemy throughout the conflict, and some areas actually prospered from this commerce. Nevertheless, the Federalists claimed that the war was ruining the economy. Some delegates to the convention advocated secession from the Union, but the majority agreed on a series of constitutional amendments to limit Republican influence, including prohibiting embargoes lasting more than sixty days and forbidding successive presidents from the same state. By the time messengers from the Hartford Convention reached Washington, D.C., however, they found the war had ended. The Hartford Convention stamped the Federalists with a stigma of disloyalty from which they never recovered.

1. New York and New England opposed war with Britain in 1812 because

   a. they felt that U.S. was not well prepared.
   b. they felt war immoral.
   c. war would interfere with commerce.
   d. they liked their Canadian neighbors.

2. The first U.S. invasion of Canada in 1812 failed, as had one during the Revolution, leaving the British in control of

   a. Detroit.
   b. Pittsburgh.
   c. Indianapolis.
   d. Cleveland.

3. During the fall of 1812 and winter of 1813, the U.S. achieved its greatest success

   a. in Detroit.
   b. in Canada.
   c. in Kentucky.
   d. at sea.

4. In September 1813, Commodore Oliver Hazard Perry won a great victory on

   a. Lake Superior.
   b. Lake Michigan.
   c. Lake Champlain.
   d. Lake Erie.

5. William Henry Harrison was able to retake _____ and penetrate into Canada.

   a. Lake Superior
   b. Lake Michigan
   c. Lake Champlain
   d. Lake Erie

6. Commodore Thomas Macdonough won a great victory in 1814 on

   a. Lake Superior.
   b. Lake Michigan.
   c. Lake Champlain.
   d. Lake Erie.

7. In 1814, the British were able to invade and set fire to

   a. Boston.
   b. New York.
   c. Baltimore.
   d. Washington, D.C.

8. The turning point of the war was the battle

   a. on Lake Erie.
   b. on Lake Champlain.
   c. at Washington, D.C.
   d. at New Orleans.

9. The Treaty of Ghent ending the war was actually signed before General Andrew Jackson's great victory

   a. on Lake Erie.
   b. on Lake Champlain.
   c. at Washington, D.C.
   d. at New Orleans.

10. Federalists from all the New England states except Maine gathered to oppose "Mr. Madison's war" in 1814 in

    a. Providence, Rhode Island.
    b. Burlington, Vermont.
    c. Boston, Massachusetts.
    d. Hartford, Connecticut.

11. The majority at the Convention favored

    a. an embargo on trade with England.
    b. secession from the Union.
    c. amendments to the Constitution.
    d. accusations of disloyalty against Federalists.

Chapter 5
Questions for Further Research

1. Assess the accomplishments and failures of the Continental Congress.

2. How did the thirteen colonies settle the question of governing themselves after declaring their independence from England?

3. Compare and explain the powers apportioned to the states and to the Continental Congress under the Articles of Confederation.

4. What was the long-term importance of the Northwest Ordinance of 1787 in providing for the development of new states, restrictions on slavery, provisions for public education, and "the utmost good faith" clause for dealing with the Native Americans in the Northwest Territory?

5. What did the states whose original charters had not granted them western lands want before they would sign the Articles of Confederation and what were the results of their demands?

6. Assess the comparative accomplishments and failures of the national government under the Articles of Confederation, and their contributions to the call for a constitutional convention to revise the Articles of Confederation.

7. What factors were involved in calling the Constitutional Convention?

8. Describe the alternative plans considered by the delegates and the major compromises agreed upon to secure the approval of the Constitution.

9. Compare the interests of those delegates who opposed and those who defended slavery, and explain the consequences of the compromises over slavery.

10. Identify the issues involved in Shays' Rebellion and present arguments from each side. Within the context of the late 18th century, were the compromises reached by the delegates to the Constitutional Convention reasonable and necessary in order to obtain approval of the Constitution?

11. What might the consequences have been had the anti-slavery delegates remained firm in their resolve?

12. Specify and explain the importance of the basic guarantees incorporated in the Bill of Rights. Which do you feel is the most important guarantee? Why?

13. Why did the Antifederalists argue for the incorporation of a Bill of Rights in the Constitution. What did they mean by a Bill of Rights? Were the Antifederalist suggestions incorporated into the Bill of Rights?

14. Compare the leaders and the social and economic composition of each of America's first two political parties.

15. Compare the different views of the two parties on the central economic and foreign policy issues of the 1790s.

16. Identify the central economic issues of the 1790s on which people with varying economic interests and regions held different views. How did these differences contribute to the development of the Federalists and the Democratic-Republicans?

17. Evaluate the role of ordinary people in the Whiskey Rebellion and in demonstrations against Jay's Treaty. What were the causes of the Whiskey Rebellion? How were the demonstrations against the whiskey tax similar to those of the revolutionary period against British taxation? What were the differences? Why did western farmers object to the Jay Treaty?

91

18. Discuss the bitterly fought presidential election of 1800, including Adams's appointment of "midnight judges." What were the issues in the election of 1800? During the campaign, why was Jefferson accused of advocating anarchy and destroying Christian principles? Was Adams's appointment of Federalist judges in the last days of his administration appropriate?

19. Identify the powers and responsibilities of the Supreme Court set forth in Article III of the Constitution and in the Judiciary Act of 1789, which confers the power of judicial review of acts of state governments.

CHAPTER 6
Westward Expansion and Regional Differences

BUILDING UNITY

The War of 1812 was, in a sense, a second war of independence, for before that time the United States had not been accorded equality in the family of nations. With its conclusion, many of the serious difficulties that the young republic had faced since the Revolution now disappeared. National union under the Constitution brought a balance between liberty and order. With a low national debt and a continent awaiting exploration, the prospect of peace, prosperity, and social progress opened before the nation.

Commerce was cementing national unity. The privations of war convinced many of the importance of protecting the manufacturers of America until they could stand alone against foreign competition. Economic independence, many argued, was as essential as political independence. To foster self-sufficiency, congressional leaders Henry Clay of Kentucky and John C. Calhoun of South Carolina urged a policy of protectionism—imposition of restrictions on imported goods to foster the development of American industry.

The time was propitious for raising the customs tariff. The shepherds of Vermont and Ohio wanted protection against an influx of English wool. In Kentucky, a new industry of weaving local hemp into cotton bagging was threatened by the Scottish bagging industry. Pittsburgh, Pennsylvania, already a flourishing center of iron smelting, was eager to challenge British and Swedish iron suppliers. The tariff enacted in 1816 imposed duties high enough to give manufacturers real protection. In addition, westerners advocated a national system of roads and canals to link them with eastern cities and ports, and to open frontier lands for settlement. However, they were unsuccessful in pressing their demands for a federal role in internal improvement because of opposition from New England and the South. Roads and canals remained the province of the states until the passage of the Federal Highways Act of 1916.

The position of the federal government at this time was greatly strengthened by several Supreme Court decisions. A committed Federalist, John Marshall of Virginia, became chief justice in 1801 and held office until his death in 1835. The court—weak before his administration—was transformed into a powerful tribunal, occupying a position co-equal to the Congress and the president. In a succession of historic decisions, Marshall never deviated from one cardinal principle: upholding the sovereignty of the Constitution.

Marshall was the first in a long line of Supreme Court justices whose decisions have molded the meaning and application of the Constitution. When he finished his long service, the court had decided nearly fifty cases clearly involving constitutional issues. In one of Marshall's most famous opinions—*Marbury* v. *Madison* (1803)—he decisively established the right of the Supreme Court to review the constitutionality of any law of Congress or of a state legislature. In *McCulloch* v. *Maryland* (1819), which dealt with the old question of the implied powers of the government under the Constitution, he stood boldly in defense of the Hamiltonian theory that the Constitution by implication gives the government powers beyond those expressly stated.

1. After the War of 1812, the United States agreed that the best way to build unity and economic independence was

   a. high protective tariffs passed in 1816.
   b. building highways.
   c. building canals.
   d. the Federal Highways Act of 1916.

2. The iron smelting center of _____ wanted to challenge British iron imports.

   a. Vermont
   b. Ohio
   c. Kentucky
   d. Pittsburgh, Pennsylvania

3. John Marshall, Chief Justice from 1801–1835, established the supremacy of

   a. Congress.
   b. state legislatures.
   c. the Supreme Court and the Constitution.
   d. implied powers.

EXTENSION OF SLAVERY

Slavery, which had up to now received little public attention, began to assume much greater importance as a national issue. In the early years of the republic, when the northern states were providing for immediate or gradual emancipation of the slaves, many leaders had supposed that slavery would die out. In 1786, George Washington wrote that he devoutly wished some plan might be adopted "by which slavery may be abolished by slow, sure and imperceptible degrees." Jefferson, Madison, and Monroe, all Virginians, and other leading southern statesmen, made similar statements. The Northwest Ordinance of 1787 had banned slavery in the Northwest Territory. As late as 1808, when the international slave trade was abolished, there were many southerners who thought that slavery would soon end. The expectation proved false, for during the next generation, the South became solidly united behind the institution of slavery as new economic factors made slavery far more profitable than it had been before 1790.

Chief among these was the rise of a great cotton-growing industry in the South, stimulated by the introduction of new types of cotton and by Eli Whitney's invention in 1793 of the cotton gin, which separated the seeds from cotton. At the same time, the Industrial Revolution, which made textile manufacturing a large-scale operation, vastly increased the demand for raw cotton. And the opening of new lands in the West after 1812 greatly extended the area available for cotton cultivation. Cotton culture moved rapidly from the Tidewater states on the east coast through much of the lower South to the delta region of the Mississippi, and eventually to Texas.
Sugarcane, another labor-intensive crop, also contributed to slavery's extension in the South. The rich, hot lands of southeastern Louisiana proved ideal for growing sugarcane profitably. By 1830, the state was supplying the nation with about half its sugar supply. Finally, tobacco growers moved westward, taking slavery with them.

As the free society of the North and the slave society of the South spread westward, it seemed politically expedient to maintain a rough equality among the new states carved out of western territories. In 1818, when Illinois was admitted to the Union, ten states permitted slavery and eleven states prohibited it; however, balance was restored after Alabama was admitted as a slave state. Population was growing faster in the North, which permitted northern states to have a clear majority in the House of Representatives. However, equality between the North and the South was maintained in the Senate.

In 1819, Missouri, which had ten thousand slaves, applied to enter the Union. Northerners rallied to oppose Missouri's entry except as a free state, and a storm of protest swept the country. For a time Congress was deadlocked, but Henry Clay arranged the so-called Missouri Compromise; Missouri was admitted as a slave state at the same time Maine came in as a free state. In addition, Congress banned slavery from the territory acquired by the Louisiana Purchase north of Missouri's southern boundary. At the time, this provision appeared to be a victory for the southern states because it was thought unlikely that this "Great American Desert" would ever be settled. The controversy was temporarily resolved, but Thomas Jefferson wrote to a friend that "this momentous question like a fireball in the night awakened me with terror. I considered it at once as the knell of the Union."

1. Slavery seemed to be on its way out until it became

    a. less acceptable.
    b. more profitable.
    c. illegal to import slaves.
    d. illegal to sell slaves.

2. The economy of the South became heavily dependent on

    a. rum.
    b. molasses.
    c. cotton.
    d. peanuts.

3. The Industrial Revolution increased the demands for raw cotton by introducing

    a. Eli Whitney's cotton gin.
    b. new types of cotton.
    c. English wool.
    d. large-scale textile manufacturing.

4. Among the labor-intensive crops that promoted slavery in the South was/were

    a. wool.
    b. iron.
    c. tobacco and sugarcane.
    d. corn and wheat.

5. The Missouri Compromise admitted

    a. Missouri as a slave state and Maine as a free state.
    b. Missouri as a free state and Maine as a slave state.
    c. Illinois and a free state and Alabama as a slave state.
    d. Illinois as a slave state and Alabama as a free state.

6. According to the Missouri Compromise, the only state north of Missouri's southern border to be admitted as a slave state was

    a. Kansas.
    b. Arkansas.
    c. Texas.
    d. Missouri.

7. The object of the Missouri Compromise of 1818 was to maintain balance between the slave and the free states in

    a. population.
    b. the House of Representatives.
    c. the Senate.
    d. Presidential elections.

8. _____ recognized that the issue of slavery would be the death knell of the Union.

    a. Henry Clay
    b. Thomas Jefferson
    c. John C. Calhoun
    d. Daniel Webster

LATIN AMERICA AND THE MONROE DOCTRINE

During the opening decades of the 19th century, Central and South America turned to revolution. The idea of liberty had stirred the people of Latin America from the time the English colonies gained their freedom. Napoleon's conquest of Spain in 1808 provided the signal for Latin Americans to rise in revolt. By 1822, ably led by Simon Bolivar, Francisco Miranda, Jose de San Martin, and Miguel Hidalgo, all of Hispanic America—from Argentina and Chile in the south to Mexico and California in the north—had won independence from the mother country.

The people of the United States took a deep interest in what seemed a repetition of their own experience in breaking away from European rule. The Latin American independence movements confirmed their own belief in self-government. In 1822, President James Monroe, under powerful public pressure, received authority to recognize the new countries of Latin America—including the former Portuguese colony of Brazil—and soon exchanged ministers with them. This recognition confirmed their status as genuinely independent countries, entirely separated from their former European connections.

At just this point, Russia, Prussia, and Austria formed an association called the Holy Alliance to protect themselves against revolution. By intervening in countries where popular movements threatened monarchies, the Alliance—joined at times by France—hoped to prevent the spread of revolution into its dominions. This policy was the antithesis of the American principle of self-determination.
As long as the Holy Alliance confined its activities to the Old World, it aroused no anxiety in the United States. But when the Alliance announced its intention of restoring its former colonies to Spain, Americans became very concerned. For its part, Britain resolved to prevent Spain from restoring its empire because trade with Latin America was too important to British commercial interests. London urged the extension of Anglo-American guarantees to Latin America, but Secretary of State John Quincy Adams convinced Monroe to act unilaterally: "It would be more candid, as well as more dignified, to avow our principles explicitly to Russia and France, than to

Reproducing copyrighted material is against the law! **96**

come in as a cock-boat in the wake of the British man-of-war." In December 1823, with the knowledge that the British navy would defend Latin America from the Holy Alliance and France, President Monroe took the occasion of his annual message to Congress to pronounce what would become known as the Monroe Doctrine—the refusal to tolerate any further extension of European domination in the Americas:

> The American continents . . . are henceforth not to be considered as subjects for future colonization by any European powers. We should consider any attempt on their part to extend their [political] system to any portion of this hemisphere as dangerous to our peace and safety. With the existing colonies or dependencies of any European power we have not interfered and shall not interfere. But with the governments who have declared their independence and maintained it, and whose independence we have . . . acknowledged, we could not view any interposition for the purpose of oppressing them, or controlling in any other manner their destiny, by any European power in any other light than as the manifestation of an unfriendly disposition toward the United States.

The Monroe Doctrine expressed a spirit of solidarity with the newly independent republics of Latin America. These nations in turn recognized their political affinity with the United States by basing their new constitutions, in many instances, on the North American model.

1. Central and South American revolutions won independence from

   a. Mexico.
   b. Chile.
   c. Argentina.
   d. Spain.

2. In addition to recognizing the independence of former Spanish colonies, in 1822, James Monroe recognized the independence of

   a. Texas.
   b. California.
   c. the former Portuguese colony of Brazil.
   d. the former Portuguese colony of Goa.

3 The Holy Alliance, formed to protect monarchies, did **not** include

   a. Great Britain.
   b. Russia.
   c. Prussia.
   d. Austria.

4. The Holy Alliance showed an interest in restoring _____ colonies in Latin America.

   a. Portuguese
   b. Spanish
   c. British
   d. French

5. _____ did not want any interference in Latin America, and wanted the United States to join with them in protecting Latin America.

   a. Great Britain
   b. France
   c. Spain
   d. Portugal

6. John Quincy Adams persuaded James Monroe to act unilaterally in proclaiming the _____ Doctrine in December 1823.

   a. Adams
   b. Jefferson
   c. Madison
   d. Monroe

7. The doctrine rejected any further _____ involvement in Latin America.

   a. British
   b. American
   c. European
   d. Asian

FACTIONALISM AND POLITICAL PARTIES

Domestically, the presidency of Monroe (1817–1825) was termed the "era of good feelings." In one sense, this term disguised a period of vigorous factional and regional conflict; on the other hand, the phrase acknowledged the political triumph of the Republican Party over the Federalist Party, which collapsed as a national force.

The decline of the Federalists brought disarray to the system of choosing presidents. At the time, state legislatures could nominate candidates. In 1824, Tennessee and Pennsylvania chose Andrew Jackson, with South Carolina Senator John C. Calhoun as his running mate. Kentucky selected Speaker of the House Henry Clay; Massachusetts, Secretary of State John Quincy Adams; and a congressional caucus, Treasury Secretary William Crawford.

Personality and sectional allegiance played important roles in determining the outcome of the election. Adams won the electoral votes from New England and most of New York; Clay won Kentucky, Ohio, and Missouri; Jackson won the Southeast, Illinois, Indiana, the Carolinas, Pennsylvania, Maryland, and New Jersey; and Crawford won Virginia, Georgia, and Delaware. No candidate gained a majority in the Electoral College, so according to the provisions of the Constitution, the election was thrown into the House of Representatives, where Clay was the most influential figure. He supported Adams, who gained the presidency.

During Adams's administration, new party alignments appeared. Adams's followers took the name of "National Republicans," later to be changed to "Whigs." Though he governed honestly and efficiently, Adams was not a popular president and his administration was marked with frustrations. Adams failed in his effort to institute a national system of roads and canals. His years in office appeared to be one long campaign for reelection, and his coldly intellectual temperament did not win friends. Jackson, by contrast, had enormous popular appeal, especially among his followers in the newly named Democratic Party that emerged from the Republican Party, with its roots dating back to presidents Jefferson, Madison, and Monroe. In the election of 1828, Jackson defeated Adams by an overwhelming electoral majority.

Jackson—Tennessee politician, Indian fighter, and hero of the Battle of New Orleans during the War of 1812—drew his support from the small farmers of the West, and the workers, artisans, and small merchants of the East, who sought to use their vote to resist the rising commercial and manufacturing interests associated with the Industrial Revolution.

The election of 1828 was a significant benchmark in the trend toward broader voter participation. Vermont had universal male suffrage from its entry into the Union and Tennessee permitted suffrage for the vast majority of taxpayers. New Jersey, Maryland, and South Carolina all abolished property and tax-paying requirements between 1807 and 1810. States entering the Union after 1815 either had universal white male suffrage or a low taxpaying requirement. From 1815 to 1821, Connecticut, Massachusetts, and New York abolished all property requirements. In 1824, members of the Electoral College were still selected by six state legislatures. By 1828, presidential electors were chosen by popular vote in every state but Delaware and South Carolina. Nothing dramatized this democratic sentiment more than the election of the flamboyant Andrew Jackson.

1. The presidency of James Monroe was called the "era of good feelings" because of the absence of

    a. regional conflict.
    b. factional conflict.
    c. organized party opposition to the Republicans.
    d. the Republican Party.

2. In 1824, among the candidates nominated for President were all of the following **except**

    a. Andrew Jackson.
    b. John C. Calhoun.
    c. Henry Clay.
    d. John Quincy Adams.

3. Treasury Secretary William Crawford, also a candidate in 1824, carried all of the following states **except**

    a. Vermont.
    b. Virginia.
    c. Georgia.
    d. Delaware.

4. John Quincy Adams won all of the following states in 1824 **except**

    a. Maine.
    b. Massachusetts.
    c. Connecticut.
    d. Kentucky.

5. Henry Clay won all of the following states in 1824 **except**

    a. Kentucky.
    b. Ohio.
    c. Missouri.
    d. Illinois.

6. Andrew Jackson won all of the following states in 1824 **except**

   a. New York.
   b. New Jersey.
   c. Pennsylvania.
   d. Indiana.

7. Since no candidate gained a majority in the Electoral College, the election was decided by

   a. the Supreme Court.
   b. the Senate.
   c. the House of Representatives.
   d. the President.

8. John Quincy Adams was elected President with the key support of

   a. William Crawford.
   b. Henry Clay.
   c. Andrew Jackson.
   d. John C. Calhoun.

9. By 1828, Andrew Jackson's party was known as the

   a. Whigs.
   b. National Republicans.
   c. Republicans.
   d. Democrats.

10. By 1828, John Quincy Adams's party was known as the

    a. Whigs.
    b. National Republicans.
    c. Republicans.
    d. Democrats.

11. In the election of 1828, _____, who had already won the popular vote in 1824, easily defeated the unpopular John Quincy Adams.

    a. Thomas Jefferson
    b. Henry Clay
    c. Andrew Jackson
    d. Daniel Webster

12. By 1828, the United States had become much more democratic, inasmuch as

    a. property taxes were lowered.
    b. presidential electors were chosen by state legislatures.
    c. most women could vote.
    d. most men could vote.

NULLIFICATION CRISIS

Toward the end of his first term in office, Jackson was forced to confront the state of South Carolina on the issue of the protective tariff. Business and farming interests in the state had hoped that Jackson would use his presidential power to modify tariff laws they had long opposed. In their view, all the benefits of protection were going to northern manufacturers, and while the country as a whole grew richer, South Carolina grew poorer, with its planters bearing the burden of higher prices.

The protective tariff passed by Congress and signed into law by Jackson in 1832 was milder than that of 1828, but it further embittered many in the state. In response, a number of South Carolina citizens endorsed the states' rights principle of "nullification," which was enunciated by John C. Calhoun, Jackson's vice president until 1832, in his *South Carolina Exposition and Protest* (1828). South Carolina dealt with the tariff by adopting the Ordinance of Nullification, which declared both the tariffs of 1828 and 1832 null and void within state borders. The legislature also passed laws to enforce the ordinance, including authorization for raising a military force and appropriations for arms.

Nullification was only the most recent in a series of state challenges to the authority of the federal government. There had been a continuing contest between the states and the national government over the power of the latter, and over the loyalty of the citizenry, almost since the founding of the republic. The Kentucky and Virginia Resolutions of 1798, for example, had defied the Alien and Sedition Acts, and in the Hartford Convention, New England voiced its opposition to President Madison and the war against the British.

In response to South Carolina's threat, Jackson sent seven small naval vessels and a man-of-war to Charleston in November 1832. On December 10th, he issued a resounding proclamation against the nullifiers. South Carolina, the president declared, stood on "the brink of insurrection and treason," and he appealed to the people of the state to reassert their allegiance to that Union for which their ancestors had fought.

When the question of tariff duties again came before Congress, it soon became clear that only one man, Senator Henry Clay, the great advocate of protection (and a political rival of Jackson), could pilot a compromise measure through Congress. Clay's tariff bill—quickly passed in 1833—specified that all duties in excess of twenty percent of the value of the goods imported were to be reduced by easy stages, so that by 1842, the duties on all articles would reach the level of the moderate tariff of 1816.

Nullification leaders in South Carolina had expected the support of other southern states, but without exception, the rest of the South declared South Carolina's course unwise and unconstitutional. Eventually, South Carolina rescinded its action. Both sides, nevertheless, claimed victory. Jackson had committed the federal government to the principle of Union supremacy. But South Carolina, by its show of resistance, had obtained many of the demands it sought, and had demonstrated that a single state could force its will on Congress.

1. The fight against high tariffs was led by Jackson's first-term vice president,

    a. James Monroe of Virginia.
    b. John Quincy Adams of Massachusetts.
    c. Martin Van Buren of New York.
    d. John C. Calhoun of South Carolina.

2. The principle of nullification had first been expressed in

   a. South Carolina's fight against tariffs in 1832.
   b. Kentucky and Virginia's fight against the Alien and Sedition Acts in 1798.
   c. New England's fight against the War of 1812 in 1814.
   d. Henry Clay's Compromise of 1833.

3. Andrew Jackson's strong stand against nullification was opposed by

   a. the northern states.
   b. the southern states.
   c. the western states.
   d. no state except South Carolina.

BATTLE OF THE BANK

Even before the nullification issue had been settled, another controversy occurred that challenged Jackson's leadership. It concerned the rechartering of the second Bank of the United States. The first bank had been established in 1791, under Alexander Hamilton's guidance, and had been chartered for a twenty-year period. Though the government held some of its stock, it was not a government bank; rather, the bank was a private corporation with profits passing to its stockholders. It had been designed to stabilize the currency and stimulate trade, but it was resented by westerners and working people who believed, along with Senator Thomas Hart Benton of Missouri, that it was a "monster" granting special favors to a few powerful men. When its charter expired in 1811, it was not renewed.

For the next few years, the banking business was in the hands of state-chartered banks, which issued currency in excessive amounts, creating great confusion and fueling inflation. It became increasingly clear that state banks could not provide the country with a uniform currency, and in 1816, a second Bank of the United States, similar to the first, was again chartered for twenty years.

From its inception, the second bank was unpopular in the newer states and territories, and with less prosperous people everywhere. Opponents claimed the bank possessed a virtual monopoly over the country's credit and currency, and reiterated that it represented the interests of the wealthy few. On the whole, the bank was well managed and rendered valuable service; but Jackson, elected as a popular champion against it, vetoed a bill to recharter the bank. In his message to Congress, he denounced monopoly and special privilege, saying that "our rich men have not been content with equal protection and equal benefits, but have besought us to make them richer by act of Congress." The effort to override the veto failed.

In the election campaign that followed, the bank question caused a fundamental division between the merchant, manufacturing, and financial interests (generally creditors who favored tight money and high interest rates), and the laboring and agrarian elements, who were often in debt to banks and therefore favored an increased money supply and lower interest rates. The outcome was an enthusiastic endorsement of "Jacksonism." Jackson saw his reelection in 1832 as a popular mandate to crush the bank irrevocably, and found a ready-made weapon in a provision of the bank's charter authorizing removal of public funds. In September 1833, he ordered that no more government money be deposited in the bank, and that the money already in its custody be gradually withdrawn in the ordinary course of meeting the expenses of government. Carefully selected state banks, stringently restricted, were provided as a substitute. For the next generation, the United States would get by on a relatively unregulated state banking system, which helped fuel westward

102

expansion through cheap credit, but kept the nation vulnerable to periodic panics. It wasn't until the Civil War that the United States chartered a national banking system.

1. Senator Thomas Hart Benton of Missouri believed that the Bank of the United States was

   a. a government bank.
   b. a force for stabilizing the currency.
   c. a "monster" granting special favors to a few.
   d. a force for stimulating trade.

2. The second Bank of the United States gained its charter in 1816 largely because of

   a. Alexander Hamilton's support.
   b. Thomas Hart Burton's support.
   c. the success of state-charted banks.
   d. the failure of state-charted banks.

3. Andrew Jackson vetoed the charter for renewal of the bank because

   a. he viewed it as a vehicle of special privilege for the rich.
   b. it was favored by the western states and the less well off.
   c. it was opposed by the merchants, bankers, and manufacturers.
   d. it was favored by laborers and farmers.

4. After being reelected in 1832, Andrew Jackson

   a. changed his mind about the bank.
   b. rechartered the bank.
   c. withdrew government money from the bank.
   d. redeposited government money in the bank.

WHIGS, DEMOCRATS, AND "KNOW-NOTHINGS"

Because Jackson's political opponents had no hope of success so long as they remained at cross purposes, they attempted to bring all the dissatisfied elements together into a common party called the Whigs. Although they organized soon after the election campaign of 1832, it was more than a decade before they reconciled their differences and were able to draw up a platform. Largely through the magnetism of Henry Clay and Daniel Webster, the Whigs' most brilliant statesmen, the party solidified its membership. However, in the 1836 election, the Whigs were still too divided to unite behind a single man or upon a common platform. New York's Martin Van Buren, Jackson's vice president, won the contest.

An economic depression and the larger-than-life personality of his predecessor obscured Van Buren's merits. His public acts aroused no enthusiasm, for he lacked the compelling qualities of leadership and the dramatic flair that had attended Jackson's every move. The election of 1840 found the country afflicted with hard times and low wages—and the Democrats on the defensive.

The Whig candidate for president was William Henry Harrison of Ohio, vastly popular as a hero of Indian conflicts as well as the War of 1812. He was regarded, like Jackson, as a representative of the democratic West. His vice presidential candidate was John Tyler, a Virginian whose views on states' rights and a low tariff were popular in the South. Harrison won a sweeping victory.

Within a month of his inauguration, however, the 68-year-old Harrison died, and Tyler became president. Tyler's beliefs differed sharply from those of Clay and Webster, still the most influential men in the country. Before Tyler's term was over, these differences led to an open break between the president and the party that had elected him.

Americans, however, found themselves divided in more complex ways than simple partisan conflicts between Whigs and Democrats. For example, the large number of Catholic immigrants in the first half of the 19th century, primarily Irish and German, triggered a backlash among native-born Protestant Americans.

Immigrants brought more than strange new customs and religious practices to American shores. They competed with the native-born population for jobs in cities along the eastern seaboard. Moreover, political changes in the 1820s and 1830s increased the political clout of the foreign-born. During those two decades, state constitutions were revised to permit universal white-male suffrage. This led to the end of rule by patrician politicians, who blamed the immigrants for their fall from power. Finally, the Catholic Church's failure to support the temperance movement gave rise to charges that Rome was trying to subvert the United States through alcohol.

The most important of the nativist organizations that sprang up in this period was a secret society, the Order of the Star-Spangled Banner, founded in 1849. When its members refused to identify themselves, they were swiftly labeled the "Know-Nothings." In 1853, the Know-Nothings in New York City organized a Grand Council, which devised a new constitution to centralize control over the state organizations.

Among the chief aims of the Know-Nothings were an extension in the period required for naturalization from five to twenty-one years, and the exclusion of the foreign-born and Catholics from public office. In 1855, the organization managed to win control of legislatures in New York and Massachusetts; by 1855, about ninety U.S. congressmen were linked to the party.

Disagreements over the slavery issue prevented the party from playing a role in national politics. The Know-Nothings of the South supported slavery while northern members opposed it. At a convention in 1856 to nominate candidates for president and vice president, forty-two northern delegates walked out when a motion to support the Missouri Compromise was ignored, and the party died as a national force.

1. The 1836 election was won by

   a. Henry Clay, a Whig.
   b. Daniel Webster, a Whig.
   c. Martin Van Buren, a Democrat.
   d. William Henry Harrison, a Whig.

2. The 1840 election, fought during hard times and low wages, was won by a popular hero from the West,

   a. Henry Clay, a Whig.
   b. Daniel Webster, a Whig.
   c. Martin Van Buren, a Democrat.
   d. William Henry Harrison, a Whig.

104

3. After only a month in office, the newly-elected President died. He was succeeded by his Vice President

   a. Henry Clay, a Whig.
   b. Daniel Webster, a Whig.
   c. Martin Van Buren, a Democrat.
   d. John Tyler, a Virginian.

4. The "Know-Nothings" were called that because they

   a. refused to identify themselves.
   b. were ignorant.
   c. were prejudiced.
   d. came from New York.

5. The Know-Nothings' main political goal was to

   a. eliminate tariffs.
   b. raise taxes.
   c. suppress immigrants and Catholics.
   d. support slavery.

STIRRINGS OF REFORM

The democratic upheaval in politics exemplified by Jackson's election was merely one phase of the long American quest for greater rights and opportunities for all citizens. Another was the beginning of labor organization. In 1835, labor forces in Philadelphia, Pennsylvania, succeeded in reducing the old "dark-to-dark" workday to a ten-hour day. New Hampshire, Rhode Island, Ohio, and the new state of California, admitted to the Union in 1850, undertook similar reforms.

The spread of suffrage had already led to a new concept of education, for clear-sighted statesmen everywhere perceived the threat to universal suffrage from an untutored, illiterate electorate. These men—DeWitt Clinton in New York, Abraham Lincoln in Illinois, and Horace Mann in Massachusetts—were now supported by organized labor, whose leaders demanded free, tax-supported schools open to all children. Gradually, in one state after another, legislation was enacted to provide for such free instruction. The public school system became common throughout the northern part of the country. In other parts of the country, however, the battle for public education continued for years.

Another influential social movement that emerged during this period was the opposition to the sale and use of alcohol, or the temperance movement. It stemmed from a variety of concerns and motives: religious beliefs, the effect of alcohol on the workforce, and the violence and suffering women and children experienced at the hands of heavy drinkers. In 1826, Boston ministers organized the Society for the Promotion of Temperance. Seven years later, in Philadelphia, the society convened a national convention, which formed the American Temperance Union. The Union called for the renunciation of all alcoholic beverages, and pressed state legislatures to ban their production and sale. Thirteen states had done so by 1855, although the laws were subsequently challenged in court. They survived only in northern New England, but between 1830 and 1860, the temperance movement reduced Americans' per capita consumption of alcohol.

Other reformers addressed the problems of prisons and care for the insane. Efforts were made to turn prisons, which stressed punishment, into penitentiaries, where the guilty would undergo rehabilitation. In Massachusetts, Dorothea Dix led a struggle to improve conditions for insane persons, who were kept confined in wretched almshouse and prisons. After winning improvements in Massachusetts, she took her campaign to the South, where nine states established hospitals for the insane between 1845 and 1852.

Such social reforms brought many women to a realization of their own unequal position in society. From colonial times, unmarried women had enjoyed many of the same legal rights as men, although custom required that they marry early. With matrimony, women virtually lost their separate identities in the eyes of the law. Women were not permitted to vote and their education in the 17th and 18th centuries was limited largely to reading, writing, music, dancing, and needlework.

The awakening of women began with the visit to America of Frances Wright, a Scottish lecturer and journalist, who publicly promoted women's rights throughout the United States during the 1820s. At a time when women were often forbidden to speak in public places, Wright not only spoke out, but shocked audiences by her views advocating the rights of women to seek information on birth control and divorce.

The early feminist, Elizabeth Cady Stanton, found an ally in Lucretia Mott, an ardent abolitionist, when the two met in 1840 at an anti-slavery conference in London. Once the conference began, it was apparent to the two women that female delegates were not welcome. Barred from speaking and appearing on the convention floor, Cady Stanton and Mott protested by leaving the convention hall, taking other female delegates with them. It was then that Cady Stanton proposed to Mott a women's rights convention that would address the social, civil, and religious rights of women. The convention would be put on hold until eight years later, when the two organized the first women's rights convention, held in Seneca Falls, New York, in 1848.

At that meeting, Cady Stanton presented a "Declaration of Sentiments," based on the Declaration of Independence, and listing eighteen grievances against male suppression of women. Among them: married women had no right to their children if they left an abusive husband or sought a divorce. If a woman was granted a divorce, there was no way for her to make a professional living unless she chose to write or teach. A woman could not testify against her husband in court. Married women who worked in factories were not entitled to keep their earnings, but had to turn them over to their husbands. When a woman married, any property that she had held as a single woman automatically became part of her husband's estate. Single women who owned property were taxed without the right to vote for the lawmakers imposing the taxes—one of the very reasons why the American colonies had broken away from Great Britain.

Convention attendees passed the resolutions unanimously with the exception of the one for women's suffrage. Only after an impassioned speech in favor of women's right to vote by Frederick Douglass, the black abolitionist, did the resolution pass. Still, the majority of those in attendance could not accept the thought of women voting.

At Seneca Falls, Cady Stanton gained national prominence as an eloquent writer and speaker for women's rights. Years later, she declared that she had realized early on that without the right to vote, women would never achieve their goal of becoming equal with men. Taking the abolitionist reformer William Lloyd Garrison as her model, she saw that the key to success in any endeavor lay in changing public opinion, and not in party action. By awakening women to the injustices under which they labored, Seneca Falls became the catalyst for future change. Soon other women's rights conventions were held, and other women would come to the forefront of the movement for political and social equality.

That same year, Ernestine Rose, a Polish immigrant, was instrumental in getting a law passed in the state of New York that allowed married women to keep their property in their own name. Among the first laws in the nation of this kind, the Married Women's Property Act, encouraged other state legislatures to enact similar laws.

In 1869, Rose helped Elizabeth Cady Stanton and another leading women's rights activist, Susan B. Anthony, to found the National Woman Suffrage Association (NWSA), which advocated a constitutional amendment for women's right to the vote. These two would become the women's movement's most outspoken advocates. Describing their partnership, Cady Stanton would say, "I forged the thunderbolts and she fired them."

1. The first fruit of the organized labor movement was

   a. health benefits.
   b. higher wages.
   c. a 10-hour workday.
   d. vacation and sick pay.

2. The leading advocates of free public education included all of the following **except**

   a. Dorothy Dix of Massachusetts.
   b. Horace Mann of Massachusetts.
   c. Abraham Lincoln of Illinois.
   d. DeWitt Clinton of New York.

3. The leading advocates of banning alcohol consumption were the _____ organizations.

   a. labor
   b. health
   c. educational
   d. Temperance

4. The leading advocate for the insane was

   a. Dorothy Dix of Massachusetts.
   b. Horace Mann of Massachusetts.
   c. Abraham Lincoln of Illinois.
   d. DeWitt Clinton of New York.

5. The leading American advocates of women's rights did **not** include

   a. Frances Wright.
   b. Elizabeth Cady Stanton.
   c. Lucretia Mott.
   d. Susan B. Anthony.

WESTWARD

The frontier did much to shape American life. Conditions along the entire Atlantic seaboard stimulated migration to the newer regions. From New England, where the soil was incapable of producing high yields of grain, came a steady stream of men and women who left their coastal farmland villages to take advantage of the rich interior land of the continent. In the backcountry settlements of the Carolinas and Virginia, people handicapped by the lack of roads and canals giving access to coastal markets, and suffering from the political dominance of the Tidewater planters, also moved westward. By 1800, the Mississippi and Ohio River valleys were becoming a great frontier region. "Hi-o, away we go, floating down the river on the O-hi-o," became the song of thousands of migrants.

The westward flow of population in the early 19th century led to the division of old territories and the drawing of new boundaries. As new states were admitted, the political map stabilized east of the Mississippi River. From 1816 to 1821, six states were created—Indiana, Illinois, and Maine (which were free states), and Mississippi, Alabama, and Missouri (slave states). The first frontier had been tied closely to Europe, the second to the coastal settlements, but the Mississippi Valley was independent and its people looked west rather than east.

Frontier settlers were a varied group. One English traveler described them as "a daring, hardy race of men, who live in miserable cabins . . . They are unpolished but hospitable, kind to strangers, honest and trustworthy. They raise a little Indian corn, pumpkins, hogs and sometimes have a cow or two . . . But the rifle is their principal means of support." Dexterous with the axe, snare, and fishing line, these men blazed the trails, built the first log cabins and confronted Native American tribes, whose land they occupied.

As more and more settlers penetrated the wilderness, many became farmers as well as hunters. A comfortable log house with glass windows, a chimney, and partitioned rooms replaced the cabin; the well replaced the spring. Industrious settlers would rapidly clear their land of timber, burning the wood for potash and letting the stumps decay. They grew their own grain, vegetables, and fruit; ranged the woods for deer, wild turkeys, and honey; fished the nearby streams; and looked after cattle and hogs. Land speculators bought large tracts of the cheap land and, if land values rose, sold their holdings and moved still farther west, making way for others.

Doctors, lawyers, storekeepers, editors, preachers, mechanics, and politicians soon followed the farmers. The farmers were the sturdy base, however. Where they settled, they intended to stay and hoped their children would remain after them. They built large barns and brick or frame houses. They brought improved livestock, plowed the land skillfully, and sowed productive seed. Some erected flour mills, sawmills, and distilleries. They laid out good highways, and built churches and schools. Incredible transformations were accomplished in a few years. In 1830, for example, Chicago, Illinois, was merely an unpromising trading village with a fort, but long before some of its original settlers had died, it had become one of the largest and richest cities in the nation.

Farms were easy to acquire. Government land after 1820 could be bought for $1.25 for about half a hectare, and after the 1862 Homestead Act, could be claimed by merely occupying and improving it. In addition, tools for working the land were easily available. It was a time when, in a phrase written by John Soule and popularized by journalist Horace Greeley, young men could "go west and grow with the country."

Except for a migration into Mexican-owned Texas, the westward march of the agricultural frontier did not pass Missouri until after 1840. In 1819, in return for assuming the claims of American

108

citizens to the amount of $5 million, the United States obtained from Spain both Florida and Spain's rights to the Oregon country in the Far West. In the meantime, the Far West had become a field of great activity in the fur trade, which was to have significance far beyond the value of the skins. As in the first days of French exploration in the Mississippi Valley, the trader was a pathfinder for the settlers beyond the Mississippi. The French and Scots-Irish trappers, exploring the great rivers and their tributaries and discovering all the passes of the Rocky and Sierra Mountains, made possible the overland migration of the 1840s and the later occupation of the interior of the nation.

Overall, the growth of the nation was enormous: the population grew from 7.25 million to more than 23 million from 1812 to 1852, and the land available for settlement increased by almost the size of Europe—from 4.4 million to 7.8 million square kilometers. Still unresolved, however, were the basic conflicts rooted in sectional differences which, by the decade of the 1860s, would explode into civil war. Inevitably, too, this westward expansion brought settlers into conflict with the original inhabitants of the land: the Indians.

In the first part of the 19th century, the most prominent figure associated with these conflicts was Andrew Jackson, the first "Westerner" to occupy the White House. In the midst of the War of 1812, Jackson, then in charge of the Tennessee militia, was sent into southern Alabama, where he ruthlessly put down an uprising of Creek Indians. The Creeks soon ceded two-thirds of their land to the United States. Jackson later routed bands of Seminole Indians from their sanctuaries in Spanish-owned Florida.

In the 1820s, President Monroe's secretary of war, John C. Calhoun, pursued a policy of removing the remaining tribes from the old Southwest and resettling them beyond the Mississippi. Jackson continued this policy as president.

In 1830, Congress passed the Indian Removal Act, providing funds to transport the eastern tribes beyond the Mississippi. In 1834, a special Indian territory was set up in what is now Oklahoma. In all, the tribes signed ninety-four treaties during Jackson's two terms, ceding millions of hectares to the federal government and removing dozens of tribes from their ancestral homelands.

Perhaps the most egregious chapter in this unfortunate history concerned the Cherokee, whose lands in western North Carolina and Georgia had been guaranteed by treaty since 1791. Among the most progressive of the eastern tribes, the Cherokees' fate was sealed when gold was discovered on their land in 1829. Even a favorable ruling from the Supreme Court proved little help. With the acquiescence of the Jackson administration, the Cherokee were forced to make the long and cruel trek to Oklahoma in 1835. Many died of disease and privation in what became known as the "Trail of Tears."

1. Andrew Jackson, then head of the Tennessee militia, put down a rising of _____ Indians during the War of 1812.

   a. Creek
   b. Seminole
   c. Cherokee
   d. Oklahoma

2. The _____ Indians were forced on a "Trail of Tears" from North Carolina and Georgia to Oklahoma.

   a. Creek
   b. Seminole
   c. Cherokee
   d. Oklahoma

3. The person most responsible for the suppression and removal of the Indians was probably

   a. John C. Calhoun.
   b. Andrew Jackson.
   c. John Soule.
   d. Horace Greeley.

Chapter 6
Questions for Further Research

1. Why is *Marbury* v. *Madison* considered a landmark decision of the Supreme Court?

2. How did Chief Justice Marshall contribute to the growth of the Supreme Court's importance in relationship to the other two branches of the federal government?

3. What were Napoleon's reasons for selling Louisiana to the United States? What would have happened if he had not sold Louisiana?

4. Compare the arguments advanced by Democratic Republicans and Federalists regarding the acquisition of Louisiana.

5. Describe President Madison's reasons for declaring war in 1812.

6. Describe the sectional divisions over the War of 1812.

7. Identify the origins and explain the provisions of the Monroe Doctrine.

8. Why did New Englanders oppose the War of 1812?

9. Why did the War Hawks want to move against Native Americans in the Northwest Territory?

10. Was the War of 1812 a "Second War for Independence," a war of expansion, or a war for maritime rights?

11. Compare the policies toward Native Americans pursued by presidential administrations from Washington to Van Buren.

12. Describe the various strategies of Native Americans, such as accommodation, revitalization, and resistance.

13. Explain why the election of Andrew Jackson was considered a victory for the "common man." What factors contributed to his election?

14. How did Jackson's veto of the U.S. Bank recharter and his actions in the nullification crisis contributed to the revolt against "King Andrew" and the rise of the Whig party? What were the political motives behind proponents and opponents of the U.S. Bank recharter? Was Jackson's position on the bank a reflection of the will of the "common man?"

15. Was Jackson or Calhoun more in line with the principles of Jefferson and Madison during the nullification crisis?

16. What might have happened if South Carolina had succeeded in nullifying the tariff?

17. Explain the Missouri Compromise and evaluate its political consequences. Why was there such bitter argument over the admission of Missouri to the Union? Why did the Missouri Compromise fail to resolve the debate over slavery? Was the compromise over the admission of Missouri an appropriate response?

18. Explain how tariff policy and issues of states' rights influenced party development and promoted sectional differences in the antebellum period (the period before the Civil War).

19. Why did certain states oppose the Wilmot Proviso? Should slavery or involuntary servitude have been permitted in territory acquired after the war with Mexico? Did Congress have the constitutional right to interfere with slavery in states where it was established? Did Congress have the right to prohibit slavery in the territories? To what extent did questions such as these inflame sectional interests?

20. Analyze the impact of the Haitian Revolution and the ending of the foreign slave trade on African Americans.

21. Explain the fundamental beliefs of abolitionism and comparing the anti-slavery positions of the "immediatists" and "gradualists" within the movement.

22. Explain the importance of the Second Great Awakening and assess the importance of its principal leaders.

23. Describe ideas concerning the individual, society, and nature expressed in the literary works of major transcendentalists.

24. Analyze the roles of women in the reform movements of education, abolition, temperance, and women's suffrage. Compare the changing roles of women of different racial, regional, and social groups.

25. Describe the background of the Seneca Falls "Declaration of Sentiments" in expressing the sentiments of women. How successful were women in gaining a redress of these grievances?

CHAPTER 7
Sectional Conflict

AMERICAN DIVERSITY

No visitor to the United States left a more enduring record of his travels and observations than the French writer and political theorist Alexis de Tocqueville, whose *Democracy in America*, first published in 1835, remains one of the most trenchant and insightful analyses of American social and political practices. Tocqueville was far too shrewd an observer to be uncritical about the United States, but his verdict was fundamentally positive. "The government of democracy brings the notion of political rights to the level of the humblest citizens," he wrote, "just as the dissemination of wealth brings the notion of property within the reach of all the members of the community." Nonetheless, Tocqueville was only one of the first of a long line of thinkers to worry whether such rough equality could survive in the face of a growing factory system that threatened to create divisions between industrial workers and a new business elite.

Other travelers marveled at the growth and vitality of the country, where they could see "everywhere the most unequivocal proofs of prosperity and rapid progress in agriculture, commerce and great public works." But such optimistic views of the American experiment were by no means universal. One skeptic was English novelist Charles Dickens, who first visited the United States in 1841–1842. "This is not the Republic I came to see," he wrote in a letter. "This is not the Republic of my imagination . . . The more I think of its youth and strength, the poorer and more trifling in a thousand respects, it appears in my eyes. In everything of which it has made a boast—excepting its education of the people, and its care for poor children—it sinks immeasurably below the level I had placed it upon."

Dickens was not alone. America in the 19th century, as throughout its history, generated expectations and passions that often did not agree with a reality that was both more mundane and more complex. Already, its size and diversity defied easy generalization and invited contradiction; America was both a freedom-loving and slave-holding society, a nation of expansive and primitive frontiers as well as cities of growing commerce and industrialization.

By 1850, the national territory stretched over forest, plain, and mountain. Within these far-flung limits dwelt 23 million people in a union comprising thirty-one states. In the East, industry boomed. In the Midwest and the South, agriculture flourished. After 1849, the gold mines of California poured a golden stream into the channels of trade.
New England and the mid-Atlantic states were the main centers of manufacturing, commerce, and finance. Principal products of these areas were textiles, lumber, clothing, machinery, leather, and woolen goods. At the same time, shipping had reached the height of its prosperity, and vessels flying the American flag plied the oceans, distributing wares of all nations.

The South, from the Atlantic to the Mississippi River and beyond, was a relatively compact political unit featuring an economy centered on agriculture. Tobacco was important to the economies of Virginia, Maryland, and North Carolina. In South Carolina, rice was an abundant crop, and the climate and soil of Louisiana encouraged the cultivation of sugar. But cotton eventually became the dominant crop and the one with which the South was identified. By 1850, the American South grew more than eighty percent of the world's cotton. Slaves were used to cultivate all these crops, though cotton most of all.

The Midwest, with its boundless prairies and swiftly growing population, flourished. Europe and the older settled parts of America demanded its wheat and meat products. The introduction of labor-saving implements—notably the McCormick reaper—made possible an unparalleled increase in farm production. The nation's wheat crops meanwhile swelled from some 35 million hectoliters in 1850 to nearly 61 million in 1860, more than half being grown in the Midwest.

An important stimulus to western prosperity was the great improvement in transportation facilities; from 1850 to 1857, the Appalachian Mountain barrier was pierced by five railway trunk lines linking the Midwest and the East. These links established the economic interests that undergirded the political alliance of the Union from 1861 to 1865. In the expansion of the railway network, the South at first had much less part. It was not until the late 1850s that a continuous line ran through the mountains connecting the lower Mississippi River with the southern Atlantic seaboard.

1. Alexis de Tocqueville thought America's biggest problem might become

    a. bringing political rights to the humblest citizens.
    b. dissemination of wealth.
    c. property within the reach of all citizens.
    d. divisions between factory workers and business owners.

2. In 1850, the main centers of manufacturing, commerce, and finance were in

    a. California and the West.
    b. New England and the Middle Atlantic states.
    c. the South.
    d. the Midwest.

3. Tobacco was important to the economics of all of the following states **except**

    a. Virginia.
    b. Maryland.
    c. Louisiana.
    d. North Carolina.

4. Rice was an abundant crop in

    a. Virginia.
    b. Maryland.
    c. South Carolina.
    d. Louisiana.

5. Sugar was an important crop in

    a. Virginia.
    b. Maryland.
    c. South Carolina.
    d. Louisiana.

6. Eventually, the dominant crop throughout the South became

    a. cotton.
    b. tobacco.
    c. rice.
    d. sugar.

7. The dominant crop in the Midwest became

   a. cotton.
   b. tobacco.
   c. rice.
   d. wheat.

8. An important economic stimulus in the 1850s was the development of

   a. the telegraph.
   b. railroads.
   c. highways.
   d. trucks.

SLAVERY AND SECTIONALISM

One issue, however, exacerbated the regional and economic differences between North and South: slavery. Resenting the large profits amassed by northern businessmen from marketing the cotton crop, southerners attributed the backwardness of their own section to northern aggrandizement. Northerners, on the other hand, declared that slavery—the "peculiar institution," which the South regarded as essential to its economy—was wholly responsible for the region's relative backwardness.

As far back as 1830, sectional lines had been steadily hardening on the slavery question. In the North, abolitionist feeling grew more and more powerful, abetted by a free-soil movement vigorously opposed to the extension of slavery into the western regions not yet organized as states. To southerners of 1850, slavery was a condition for which they felt no more responsible than for their English speech or their representative institutions. In some seaboard areas, slavery by 1850 was well over two hundred years old; it was an integral part of the basic economy of the region.

Only a minority of southern whites owned slaves. In 1860, there were a total of 46,274 planters throughout the slave-holding states, with a planter defined as someone who owned at least twenty slaves. More than half of all slaves worked on plantations. Some of the yeoman farmers, seventy percent of whom held less than forty hectares, had a handful of slaves, but most had none. The "poor whites" lived on the lowest rung of southern society and held no slaves. It is easy to understand the interest of the planters in slave holding—they owned most of the slaves—but the yeomen and poor whites supported the institution of slavery as well. They feared that if freed, blacks would compete with them for land. Equally important, the presence of slaves raised the standing of the yeomen and the poor whites on the social scale; they would not willingly relinquish this status.

As they fought the weight of northern opinion, political leaders of the South, the professional classes, and most of the clergy now no longer apologized for slavery but championed it. Southern publicists insisted, for example, that the relationship between capital and labor was more humane under the slavery system than under the wage system of the North.

Before 1830, the old patriarchal system of plantation government, with its personal supervision of the slaves by their masters, was still characteristic. Gradually, however, with the introduction of large-scale cotton production in the lower South, the master gradually ceased to exercise close personal supervision over his slaves, and employed professional overseers whose tenure depended

114

upon their ability to exact from slaves a maximum amount of work.

Slavery was inherently a system of brutality and coercion in which beatings and the breakup of families through the sale of individuals were commonplace. In the end, however, the most trenchant criticism of slavery was not the behavior of individual masters and overseers toward the slaves, but slavery's fundamental violation of every human being's inalienable right to be free.

In national politics, southerners chiefly sought protection and enlargement of the interests represented by the cotton-slavery system. Expansion was considered a necessity because the wastefulness of cultivating a single crop, cotton, rapidly exhausted the soil, increasing the need for new fertile lands. Moreover, the South believed it needed new territory for additional slave states to offset the admission of new free states. Anti-slavery northerners saw in the southern view a conspiracy for proslavery aggrandizement, and their opposition became fierce in the 1830s.

An earlier anti-slavery movement, an offshoot of the American Revolution, had won its last victory in 1808 when Congress abolished the slave trade with Africa. Thereafter, opposition was largely by the Quakers, who kept up a mild but ineffectual protest, while the cotton gin and westward expansion into the Mississippi delta region were creating an increasing demand for slaves.

The abolitionist movement that emerged in the early 1830s was combative, uncompromising, and insistent upon an immediate end to slavery. This approach found a leader in William Lloyd Garrison, a young man from Massachusetts, who combined the heroism of a martyr with the crusading zeal of a demagogue. On January 1, 1831, Garrison produced the first issue of his newspaper, *The Liberator*, which bore the announcement: "I shall strenuously contend for the immediate enfranchisement of our slave population. . . . On this subject I do not wish to think, or speak, or write with moderation . . . I am in earnest—I will not equivocate—I will not excuse—I will not retreat a single inch AND I WILL BE HEARD."

Garrison's sensational methods awakened northerners to the evil in an institution many had long come to regard as unchangeable. He sought to hold up to public gaze the most repulsive aspects of slavery and to castigate slaveholders as torturers and traffickers in human life. He recognized no rights of the masters, acknowledged no compromise, tolerated no delay. Other abolitionists, unwilling to subscribe to his law-defying tactics, held that reform should be accomplished by legal and peaceful means. Garrison was joined by another powerful voice, that of Frederick Douglass, an escaped slave who galvanized northern audiences as a spokesman for the Massachusetts Anti-Slavery Society, and later as the eloquent editor of the abolitionist weekly newspaper, *Northern Star*.

One phase of the anti-slavery movement involved helping slaves escape to safe refuges in the North or over the border into Canada. Known as the "Underground Railroad," an elaborate network of secret routes was firmly established in the 1830s in all parts of the North, with its most successful operation being in the old Northwest Territory. In Ohio alone, it is estimated that from 1830 to 1860 no fewer than forty thousand fugitive slaves were helped to freedom. The number of local anti-slavery societies increased at such a rate that by 1840 there were about two thousand with a membership of perhaps 200,000.

Despite the efforts of active abolitionists to make slavery a question of conscience, most northerners held themselves aloof from the anti-slavery movement or actively opposed it. In 1837, for example, a mob attacked and killed the anti-slavery editor Elijah P. Lovejoy in Alton, Illinois. Nevertheless, certain southern actions allowed the abolitionists to link the slavery issue with the cause of civil liberties for whites. In 1835, an angry mob destroyed abolitionist literature in the Charleston, South Carolina, post office. When the postmaster stated he would not enforce delivery of abolitionist material, bitter debates ensued in Congress. In addition, abolitionists decided to flood Congress with petitions calling for a ban on slavery in the District of Columbia. In 1836, the House voted to table such petitions automatically, thus effectively killing them. Former President John Quincy Adams, elected to the House of Representatives in 1830, fought this so-called "gag rule" as a violation of the First Amendment. The House repealed the gag rule in 1844.

1. Why did small landowners and poor whites in the South support slavery?

    a. tradition
    b. religion
    c. status and fear of competition
    d. moral leadership

2. Southerners wanted to expand the cotton-slavery system to other areas for all of the following reasons **except**

    a. cotton rapidly exhausted the soil.
    b. they needed new fertile land.
    c. they were importing new slaves.
    d. they wanted to offset the North's political power.

3. The first combative voice against slavery, the editor of *The Liberator*, was

    a. William Lloyd Garrison.
    b. Frederick Douglass.
    c. Elijah Lovejoy.
    d. the Quakers.

4. John Quincy Adams, the former President, led abolitionists fighting against the

    a. Massachusetts Anti-Slavery Society.
    b. Underground Railroad.
    c. ban on slavery in Washington, D.C.
    d. "gag rule."

TEXAS AND WAR WITH MEXICO

Throughout the 1820s, Americans settled in the vast territory of Texas, often with land grants from the Mexican government. Their numbers soon alarmed the authorities, however, who prohibited further immigration in 1830. In 1834, General Antonio Lopez de Santa Anna established a dictatorship in Mexico, and the following year Texans revolted. Santa Anna defeated the American rebels at the celebrated siege of the Alamo in early 1836, but Texans under Sam Houston destroyed the Mexican army and captured Santa Anna a month later at the Battle of San Jacinto, ensuring Texan independence. For almost a decade, Texas remained an independent republic, becoming the twenty-eighth state in 1845.

Although Mexico broke relations with the United States over the issue of Texas statehood, the most contentious issue was the new state's border: Texas claimed the Rio Grande River; Mexico argued that the border stood far to the north along the Nueces River. Meanwhile, settlers were flooding into the territories of New Mexico and California at a time when many Americans claimed that the United States had a "manifest destiny" to expand westward to the Pacific Ocean.

U.S. attempts to buy the New Mexico and California territories failed, and after a clash of Mexican and U.S. troops along the Rio Grande, the United States declared war in 1846. U.S. forces occupied the territory of New Mexico, then supported the revolt of settlers in California. A U.S. force under Zachary Taylor invaded Mexico, winning victories at Monterey and Buena Vista, but failing to bring Mexico to the negotiating table. In March 1847, U.S. forces commanded by Winfield Scott landed near Vera Cruz on Mexico's east coast, and after a series of heavy engagements, entered Mexico City. Nevertheless, it was only after the resignation of Santa Anna that the United States was able to negotiate the Treaty of Guadalupe Hildago in which Mexico ceded the southwest region and California for $15 million.

The war proved to be a training ground for American officers, who would later fight on both sides in the Civil War. It was also a politically divisive war in which anti-slavery Whigs criticized the Democratic administration of James K. Polk for expansionism.

With the conclusion of the Mexican War, the United States gained a vast new territory of 1.36 million square kilometers encompassing the present-day states of Arizona, Nevada, California, Utah, and parts of New Mexico, Colorado, and Wyoming. But it was also a poisoned acquisition because it revived the most explosive question in American politics of the time: would the new territories be slave or free?

1. Texas revolted against Santa Anna's rule in Mexico in

    a. 1830.
    b. 1834.
    c. 1835.
    d. 1836.

2. Texas became independent after _____ won the battle of San Jacinto in 1836.

    a. the Alamo
    b. General Santa Anna
    c. Stephen Austin
    d. Sam Houston

3. Texas became a state in

    a. 1835.
    b. 1845.
    c. 1846.
    d. 1847.

4. Mexico claimed that Texas' southern border should be the

    a. Nueces River.
    b. Colorado River.
    c. Rio Grande.
    d. Red River.

5. The United States went to war with Mexico in 1846 after

    a. invading Mexico.
    b. invading California.
    c. failing to buy New Mexico and California.
    d. Mexico invaded California.

6. California won its independence when

    a. Zachary Taylor invaded.
    b. Winfield Scott invaded.
    c. the settlers revolted.
    d. Santa Anna revolted.

7. Winfield Scott brought Mexico to its knees after

    a. beating Zachary Taylor at Monterey.
    b. beating Zachary Taylor at Buena Vista.
    c. conquering Vera Cruz.
    d. entering Mexico City.

8. After Santa Anna resigned in 1847, the new government of Mexico agreed to

    a. grant Texas independence.
    b. sell the Louisiana Purchase.
    c. cede the Southwest and California to the U.S. for $15 million.
    d. sell Alaska to the U.S.

THE COMPROMISE OF 1850

Until 1845, it had seemed likely that slavery would be confined to the areas where it already existed. It had been given limits by the Missouri Compromise in 1820 and had no opportunity to overstep them. The new territories made renewed expansion of slavery a real likelihood.

Many northerners believed that if not allowed to spread, slavery would ultimately decline and die. To justify their opposition to adding new slave states, they pointed to the statements of Washington and Jefferson, and to the Ordinance of 1787, which forbade the extension of slavery into the Northwest. Texas, which already permitted slavery, naturally entered the Union as a slave state. However, California, New Mexico, and Utah did not have slavery, and when the United States prepared to take over these areas in 1846, there were conflicting suggestions on what to do with them.

Extremists in the South urged that all the lands acquired from Mexico be thrown open to slaveholders. Anti-slavery northerners, on the other hand, demanded that all the new regions be closed to slavery. One group of moderates suggested that the Missouri Compromise line be extended to the Pacific with free states north of it and slave states to the south. Another group proposed that the question be left to "popular sovereignty"; that is, the government should permit settlers to enter the new territory with or without slaves as they pleased and, when the time came to organize the region into states, the people themselves should determine the question.

Southern opinion held that all the territories had the right to sanction slavery. The North asserted that no territories had the right. In 1848, nearly 300,000 men voted for the candidates of a Free Soil Party, who declared that the best policy was "to limit, localize and discourage slavery." The midwestern and border state regions—Maryland, Kentucky, Missouri—were even more divided, however, with many favoring popular sovereignty as a compromise.

In January 1848, the discovery of gold in California precipitated a headlong rush of more than eighty thousand settlers for the single year of 1849. California became a crucial question, for clearly Congress had to determine the status of this new region before an organized government could be established. The hopes of the nation rested with Senator Henry Clay, who twice before in times of crisis had come forward with compromise arrangements. Now once again he halted a dangerous sectional quarrel with a complicated and carefully balanced plan.

His compromise (as subsequently modified in Congress) contained a number of key provisions: that California be admitted as a state with a free-soil (slavery-prohibited) constitution; that the remainder of the new annexation be divided into the two territories of New Mexico and Utah and organized without mention of slavery; that the claims of Texas to a portion of New Mexico be satisfied by a payment of $10 million; that more effective machinery be established for catching runaway slaves and returning them to their masters; and that the buying and selling of slaves (but not slavery) be abolished in the District of Columbia. These measures known in American history as the Compromise of 1850 were passed, and the country breathed a sigh of relief.

For three years, the compromise seemed to settle nearly all differences. Beneath the surface, however, tension grew. The new Fugitive Slave Law deeply offended many northerners, who refused to have any part in catching slaves. Moreover, many northerners continued to help fugitives escape, and made the Underground Railroad more efficient and more daring than it had been before.

1. After the war with Mexico, the principal issue surrounding the newly acquired territories was

   a. Indian rights.
   b. mining rights.
   c. water rights.
   d. slavery.

2. Extremists in the South wanted

   a. all land acquired from Mexico open to slave owners.
   b. all new regions closed to slavery.
   c. the Missouri Compromise line extended to the Pacific.
   d. popular sovereignty.

3. Anti-slavery northerners wanted

   a. all land acquired from Mexico open to slave owners.
   b. all new regions closed to slavery.
   c. the Missouri Compromise line extended to the Pacific.
   d. popular sovereignty.

4. Many in midwestern and border states such as Maryland, Kentucky, and Missouri favored

   a. all land acquired from Mexico open to slave owners.
   b. all new regions closed to slavery.
   c. the Missouri Compromise line extended to the Pacific.
   d. popular sovereignty.

5. California became the center of controversy because

   a. it was furthest away from Washington.
   b. it had the highest mountains.
   c. the gold rush of 1849 had vastly increased its population.
   d. it was still independent.

6. The issue of slavery in the new territories was resolved by the Great Compromiser, _____, and his Compromise of 1850.

   a. Thomas Jefferson
   b. Henry Clay
   c. Daniel Webster
   d. John C. Calhoun

7. The most obnoxious feature of the Compromise of 1850 to many northerners was

   a. the new territories of New Mexico and Utah.
   b. the payment of $10 million to Texas.
   c. the Underground Railroad.
   d. the Fugitive Slave Law.

A DIVIDED NATION

Politically, the 1850s can be characterized as a decade of failure in which the nation's leaders were unable to resolve, or even contain, the divisive issue of slavery. In 1852, for example, Harriet Beecher Stowe published *Uncle Tom's Cabin*, a novel provoked by the passage of the Fugitive Slave Law. When Stowe began writing her book, she thought of it as only a minor sketch, but it widened in scope as the work progressed. Immediately upon its publication, it caused a sensation. More than 300,000 copies were sold the first year, and presses ran day and night to keep up with the demand.

Although sentimental and full of stereotypes, *Uncle Tom's Cabin* portrayed with undeniable force the cruelty of slavery and the fundamental conflict between free and slave societies. The rising generation of voters in the North was deeply stirred by the work. It inspired widespread enthusiasm for the anti-slavery cause, appealing as it did to basic human emotions—indignation at injustice and pity for the helpless individuals exposed to ruthless exploitation.

In 1854, the old issue of slavery in the territories was renewed and the quarrel became more bitter. The region that now comprises Kansas and Nebraska was being rapidly settled, increasing pressure for the establishment of territorial, and eventually, state governments.

Under terms of the Missouri Compromise of 1820, the entire region was closed to slavery. The Compromise of 1850, however, inadvertently reopened the question. Dominant slaveholding elements in Missouri objected to letting Kansas become a free territory, for their state would then have three free-soil neighbors (Illinois, Iowa, and Kansas). They feared the prospect of their state being forced to become a free state as well. For a time, Missourians in Congress, backed by southerners, blocked all efforts to organize the region.

At this point, Stephen A. Douglas, the Democratic senior senator from Illinois, stirred up a storm by proposing a bill, the Kansas-Nebraska Act, which enraged all free-soil supporters. Douglas argued that the Compromise of 1850, which left Utah and New Mexico free to resolve the slavery issue for themselves, superseded the Missouri Compromise. His plan called for two territories, Kansas and Nebraska, and permitted settlers to carry slaves into them. The inhabitants themselves were to determine whether they should enter the Union as free or slave states.

Northerners accused Douglas of currying favor with the South in order to gain the presidency in 1856. Angry debates marked the progress of the bill. The free-soil press violently denounced it. Northern clergymen assailed it. Businessmen who had hitherto befriended the South suddenly turned about-face. Yet in May 1854, the Kansas-Nebraska Act passed the Senate amid the boom of cannon fired by southern enthusiasts. When Douglas subsequently visited Chicago to speak in his own defense, the ships in the harbor lowered their flags to half-mast, the church bells tolled for an hour and a crowd of ten thousand hooted so loudly that he could not make himself heard.

The immediate results of Douglas's ill-starred measure were momentous. The Whig Party, which had straddled the question of slavery expansion, sank to its death, and in its stead a powerful new organization arose, the Republican Party, whose primary demand was that slavery be excluded from all the territories. In 1856, it nominated John Fremont, whose expeditions into the Far West had won him renown. Although Fremont lost the election, the new Republican Party swept a great part of the North. Such free-soil leaders as Salmon P. Chase and William Seward exerted greater influence than ever. Along with them appeared a tall, lanky Illinois attorney, Abraham Lincoln.

The flow of both southern slaveholders and anti-slavery families into Kansas resulted in armed conflict, and soon the territory was being called "bleeding Kansas." Other events brought the nation still closer to upheaval: notably, the Supreme Court's infamous 1857 decision concerning Dred Scott.

Scott was a Missouri slave who, some twenty years earlier, had been taken by his master to live in Illinois and the Wisconsin Territory, where slavery had been banned by the Northwest Ordinance. Returning to Missouri and becoming discontented with his life there, Scott sued for liberation on the ground of his residence on free soil. The Supreme Court—dominated by southerners—decided that Scott lacked standing in court because he was not a citizen; that the laws of a free state (Illinois) had no effect on his status because he was the resident of a slave state (Missouri); and that slaveholders had the right to take their "property" anywhere in the federal territories and that Congress could not restrict the expansion of slavery. The Court's decision thus invalidated the whole set of comprise measures by which Congress for a generation had tried to settle the slavery issue.

The Dred Scott decision stirred fierce resentment throughout the North. Never before had the court been so bitterly condemned. For southern Democrats, the decision was a great victory, since it gave judicial sanction to their justification of slavery throughout the territories.

Abraham Lincoln had long regarded slavery as an evil. In a speech in Peoria, Illinois, in 1854, he declared that all national legislation should be framed on the principle that slavery was to be restricted and eventually abolished. He contended also that the principle of popular sovereignty was false, for slavery in the western territories was the concern not only of the local inhabitants but of the United States as a whole. This speech made him widely known throughout the growing West.

In 1858, Lincoln opposed Stephen A. Douglas for election to the U.S. Senate from Illinois. In the first paragraph of his opening campaign speech, on June 17th, Lincoln struck the keynote of American history for the seven years to follow:

> A house divided against itself cannot stand. I believe this government cannot endure permanently half slave and half free. I do not expect the Union to be dissolved—I do not expect the house to fall—but I do expect it will cease to be divided.

Lincoln and Douglas engaged in a series of seven debates in the ensuing months of 1858. Senator Douglas, known as the "Little Giant," had an enviable reputation as an orator, but he met his match in Lincoln, who eloquently challenged the concept of popular sovereignty as defined by Douglas and his allies. In the end, Douglas won the election by a small margin, but Lincoln had achieved stature as a national figure.

Sectional strife was growing ever more acute. On the night of October 16, 1859, John Brown, an anti-slavery fanatic who had captured and killed five proslavery settlers in Kansas three years before, led a band of followers in an attack on the federal arsenal at Harper's Ferry in what is now the state of West Virginia. Brown's goal was to use the weapons seized to lead a slave uprising. After two days of fighting, Brown and his surviving men were taken prisoner by a force of U.S. marines commanded by Colonel Robert E. Lee.

Alarm ran through the nation. For many southerners, Brown's attempt confirmed their worst fears. Anti-slavery zealots, on the other hand, hailed Brown as a martyr to a great cause. Most northerners repudiated his deed, seeing in it an assault on law and order. Brown was tried for conspiracy, treason, and murder, and on December 2, 1859, he was hanged. To the end, he believed he had been an instrument in the hand of God.

1. Readers in the North became even more emphatic and unanimous in their opposition to slavery as a result of the publication of

   a. the Ordinance of 1787.
   b. the Missouri Compromise of 1820.
   c. the Fugitive Slave Law.
   d. Harriet Beecher Stowe's *Uncle Tom's Cabin*.

2. After the Compromise of 1850, which of the following states was dominated by slaveholding elements?

   a. Illinois
   b. Missouri
   c. Kansas
   d. Nebraska

3. After the Compromise of 1850, _____ became a bone of contention between pro-slavery and free-soil advocates.

   a. Missouri
   b. Kansas
   c. Iowa
   d. Louisiana

4. The Kansas-Nebraska Act of 1854

   a. did not permit slaves in either territory.
   b. permitted slaves in both territories, subject to votes of their citizens.
   c. permitted slaves in Kansas, but not Nebraska.
   d. permitted slaves in Nebraska, but not Kansas.

5. The sponsor of the Kansas-Nebraska Act, _____, became extremely unpopular in the North.

   a. Stephen Douglas
   b. John Fremont
   c. William Seward
   d. Abraham Lincoln

6. The new Republican Party succeeded the Whigs. While extremely popular in the North as the free soil party, its candidate _____ lost the election of 1856.

   a. Stephen Douglas
   b. John Fremont
   c. William Seward
   d. Abraham Lincoln

7. The Kansas-Nebraska Act of 1854 led to violence and strife in

   a. Missouri
   b. Kansas
   c. Nebraska
   d. Louisiana

8. The supreme court in 1857 decided that Dred Scott's status was decided by the fact that he was a resident of the slave state,

    a. Wisconsin.
    b. Illinois.
    c. Ohio.
    d. Missouri.

9. The court held that Dred Scott

    a. was a citizen.
    b. was free in a free state.
    c. had no standing to sue.
    d. was no longer property.

10. Abraham Lincoln became widely known in the West for a speech he made in Peoria, Illinois in 1854, declaring

    a. slavery should be unrestricted.
    b. slavery should be abolished immediately.
    c. slavery should not be allowed in new territories.
    d. popular sovereignty should apply in new territories.

11. Stephen Douglas and Abraham Lincoln fought an election in 1858 for the

    a. U.S. Senate.
    b. U.S. House of Representatives.
    c. Governorship of Illinois.
    d. State Senate in Illinois.

12. "A house divided against itself cannot stand" was said by

    a. Stephen Douglas.
    d. Abraham Lincoln.
    c. John Brown.
    d. Robert E. Lee.

13. The winner of the 1858 election was

    a. Stephen Douglas.
    d. Abraham Lincoln.
    c. John Brown.
    d. Robert E. Lee.

14. A violent anti-slavery fanatic from Kansas, _____ led a raid on Harper's Ferry in 1859, hoping to lead a slave uprising.

    a. Stephen Douglas
    d. Abraham Lincoln
    c. John Brown
    d. Robert E. Lee

15. The Harper's Ferry raiders were taken prisoner by _____, and the leader later hung.

    a. Stephen Douglas
    d. Abraham Lincoln
    c. John Brown
    d. Robert E. Lee

SECESSION AND CIVIL WAR

In the presidential election of 1860, the Republican Party nominated Abraham Lincoln as its candidate. Party spirit soared as leaders declared that slavery could spread no farther. The party also promised a tariff for the protection of industry and pledged the enactment of a law granting free homesteads to settlers who would help in the opening of the West. The Democrats were not united. Southerners split from the party and nominated Vice President John C. Breckenridge of Kentucky for president. Stephen A. Douglas was the nominee of northern Democrats. Diehard Whigs from the border states, formed into the Constitutional Union Party, nominated John C. Bell of Tennessee.

Lincoln and Douglas competed in the North, and Breckenridge and Bell in the South. Lincoln won only thirty-nine percent of the popular vote, but had a clear majority of one hundred and eighty electoral votes, carrying all eighteen free states. Bell won Tennessee, Kentucky, and Virginia; Breckenridge took the other slave states except for Missouri, which was won by Douglas. Despite his poor electoral showing, Douglas trailed only Lincoln in the popular vote.

Lincoln's election made South Carolina's secession from the Union a foregone conclusion. The state had long been waiting for an event that would unite the South against the anti-slavery forces. Once the election returns were certain, a special South Carolina convention declared "that the Union now subsisting between South Carolina and other states under the name of the 'United States of America' is hereby dissolved." By February 1, 1861, six more southern states had seceded. On February 7th, the seven states adopted a provisional constitution for the Confederate States of America. The remaining southern states as yet remained in the Union.

Less than a month later, on March 4, 1861, Abraham Lincoln was sworn in as president of the United States. In his inaugural address, he refused to recognize the secession, considering it "legally void." His speech closed with a plea for restoration of the bonds of union. But the South turned deaf ears, and on April 12th, guns opened fire on the federal troops stationed at Fort Sumter in the Charleston, South Carolina, harbor. A war had begun in which more Americans would die than in any other conflict before or since.

In the seven states that had seceded, the people responded promptly to the appeal of the new president of the Confederate States of America, Jefferson Davis. Both sides now tensely awaited the action of the slave states that thus far had remained loyal. In response to the shelling of Fort Sumter, Virginia seceded on April 17th, and Arkansas, Tennessee, and North Carolina followed quickly. No state left the Union with greater reluctance than Virginia. Her statesmen had a leading part in the winning of the Revolution and the framing of the Constitution, and she had provided the nation with five presidents. With Virginia went Colonel Robert E. Lee, who declined the command of the Union Army out of loyalty to his state. Between the enlarged Confederacy and the free-soil North lay the border states of Delaware, Maryland, Kentucky, and Missouri which, despite some sympathies with the South, remained loyal to the Union.

Each side entered the war with high hopes for an early victory. In material resources the North enjoyed a decided advantage. Twenty-three states with a population of 22 million were arrayed against eleven states inhabited by 9 million. The industrial superiority of the North exceeded even its preponderance in population, providing it with abundant facilities for manufacturing arms and ammunition, clothing, and other supplies. Similarly, the network of railways in the North enhanced federal military prospects.

The South had certain advantages as well. The most important was geography; the South was fighting a defensive war on its own territory. The South also had a stronger military tradition, and hence the region initially boasted the more experienced military leaders.

1. The Republican Party of 1860 did **not** advocate

    a. halting the spread of slavery.
    b. a protective tariff.
    c. free homesteads in the West.
    d. an immediate end to slavery.

2. In 1860, the southern Democrats supported

    a. Abraham Lincoln.
    b. John Breckenridge.
    c. Stephen Douglas.
    d. John C. Bell.

3. The northern Democrats supported

    a. Abraham Lincoln.
    b. John Breckenridge.
    c. Stephen Douglas.
    d. John C. Bell.

4. The Whigs, or Constitutional Union Party supported _____, who carried Tennessee, Kentucky, and Virginia.

    a. Abraham Lincoln.
    b. John Breckenridge.
    c. Stephen Douglas.
    d. John C. Bell.

5. Missouri was the only state carried by _____, even though he came in second in the popular vote.

    a. Abraham Lincoln.
    b. John Breckenridge.
    c. Stephen Douglas.
    d. John C. Bell.

6. _____ won most of the southern slave states.

    a. Abraham Lincoln
    b. John Breckenridge
    c. Stephen Douglas
    d. John C. Bell

7. The overall winner of the 1860 election, who claimed all 18 free states, was

   a. Abraham Lincoln.
   b. John Breckenridge.
   c. Stephen Douglas.
   d. John C. Bell.

8. In reaction to Lincoln's election, _____ was the first state to secede.

   a. Virginia
   b. South Carolina
   c. Arkansas
   d. North Carolina

9. The Civil War started on ____, when southern guns opened fire on the federal troops in Fort Sumter, Charleston, South Carolina.

   a. February 1, 1861
   b. February 7, 1861
   c. March 4, 1861
   d. April 12, 1861

10. After Fort Sumter was shelled, four more slave states joined the original seven, the most reluctant of which was

    a. Virginia.
    b. South Carolina.
    c. Arkansas.
    d. North Carolina.

11. The command of the Union Army was offered to _____, who declined out of loyalty to Virginia.

    a. Jefferson Davis
    b. John C. Breckenridge
    c. Robert E. Lee
    d. Stephen Douglas

12. Which of the following border states joined the Confederacy?

    a. Delaware
    b. Maryland
    c. Tennessee
    d. Kentucky

13. Which of the following slave states remained loyal to the Union?

    a. Arkansas
    b. Virginia
    c. North Carolina
    d. Missouri

14. The northern states had all of the following advantages **except**

    a. geography and tradition.
    b. material resources.
    c. population.
    d. industry.

WESTERN ADVANCE, EASTERN STALEMATE

The first large battle of the war, at Bull Run, Virginia, (also known as First Manassas) near Washington, stripped away any illusions that victory would be quick or easy. It also established a pattern, at least in the eastern United States, of bloody southern victories, but victories that never translated into a decisive military advantage. For the first years, the South would often win the battle, but not the war.

In contrast to its military failures in the East, Union forces were able to secure battlefield victories and slow strategic success at sea and in the West. Most of the navy, at the war's beginning, was in Union hands, but it was scattered and weak. Secretary of the Navy Gideon Welles took prompt measures to strengthen it. Lincoln then proclaimed a blockade of the southern coasts. Although the effect of the blockade was negligible at first, by 1863 it almost completely prevented shipments of cotton to Europe and the importation of munitions, clothing, and the medical supplies the South sorely needed.

Meanwhile, a brilliant naval commander, David Farragut, conducted two remarkable operations. In one, he took a Union fleet into the mouth of the Mississippi River, where he forced the surrender of the largest city in the South, New Orleans, Louisiana. In another, he made his way past the fortified entrance of Mobile Bay, Alabama, captured a Confederate ironclad vessel, and sealed up the port.

In the Mississippi Valley, the Union forces won an almost uninterrupted series of victories. They began by breaking a long Confederate line in Tennessee, thus making it possible to occupy almost all the western part of the state. When the important Mississippi River port of Memphis was taken, Union troops advanced some three hundred and twenty kilometers into the heart of the Confederacy. With the tenacious General Ulysses S. Grant in command, Union forces withstood a sudden Confederate counterattack at Shiloh, on the bluffs overlooking the Tennessee River, holding their ground stubbornly until reinforcements arrived to repulse the Confederates. Those killed and wounded at Shiloh numbered more than ten thousand on each side, a casualty rate that Americans had never before experienced. But it was only the beginning of the carnage.

In Virginia, by contrast, Union troops continued to meet one defeat after another. In a succession of bloody attempts to capture Richmond, the Confederate capital, Union forces were repeatedly thrown back. The Confederates had two great advantages: strong defense positions afforded by numerous streams cutting the road between Washington and Richmond; and two generals, Robert E. Lee and Thomas J. ("Stonewall") Jackson, each of whom far surpassed in ability the early Union commanders. In 1862, the Union commander, George McClellan, made a slow, excessively cautious attempt to seize Richmond. But in the Seven Days' Battles between June 25th and July 1st, the Union troops were driven steadily backward, both sides suffering terrible losses.

After another Confederate victory at the Second Battle of Bull Run (or Second Manassas), Lee crossed the Potomac River and invaded Maryland. McClellan again responded tentatively, despite learning that Lee had split his army and was heavily outnumbered. The Union and Confederate

Armies met at Antietam Creek, near Sharpsburg, Maryland, on September 17, 1862, in the bloodiest single day of the war. More than four thousand died on both sides and eighteen thousand were wounded. Despite his numerical advantage, however, McClellan failed to break Lee's lines or press the attack, and Lee was able to retreat across the Potomac with his army intact. As a result, Lincoln fired McClellan.

Although Antietam was inconclusive in military terms, its consequences were nonetheless momentous. Great Britain and France, both on the verge of recognizing the Confederacy, delayed their decision, and the South never received the diplomatic recognition and economic aid from Europe that it desperately sought.

Antietam also gave Lincoln the opening he needed to issue the preliminary Emancipation Proclamation, which declared that as of January 1, 1863, all slaves in states rebelling against the Union were free. In practical terms, the Proclamation had little immediate impact; it freed slaves only in the Confederate states, while leaving slavery intact in the border states. Politically, however, it meant that in addition to preserving the Union, the abolition of slavery was now a declared objective of the Union war effort.

The final Emancipation Proclamation, issued January 1, 1863, also authorized the recruitment of blacks into the Union Army, which abolitionist leaders such as Frederick Douglass had been urging since the beginning of armed conflict. In fact, Union forces already had been sheltering escaped slaves as "contraband of war," but following the Emancipation Proclamation, the Union Army recruited and trained regiments of black soldiers that fought with distinction in battles from Virginia to the Mississippi. About 178,000 African Americans served in the United States Colored Troops, and 29,500 blacks served in the Union Navy.

Despite the political gains represented by the Emancipation Proclamation, however, the North's military prospects in the East remained as bleak as Lee's Army of Northern Virginia continued to maul the Union Army of the Potomac, first at Fredericksburg, Virginia, in December 1862 and then at Chancellorsville in May 1863. But Chancellorsville, although one of Lee's most brilliant military victories, was also one of his most costly with the death of his most valued lieutenant, General Stonewall Jackson, who was mistakenly shot by his own men.

1. The first battle of the Civil War, Bull Run or First Manassas, resulted in

    a. a decisive military advantage to the South.
    b. a decisive military advantage to the North.
    c. a bloody but indecisive southern victory.
    d. a bloody but indecisive northern victory.

2. The naval commander, David Farragut, forced the surrender of the South's largest city,

    a. Mobile, Alabama.
    b. New Orleans, Louisiana.
    c. Charleston, South Carolina.
    d. Richmond, Virginia.

3. Union forces won important battles in the _____ valley.

    a. Shenandoah
    b. Ohio
    c. Potomac
    d. Mississippi

4. Victory in the West was assured when General _____ withstood a Confederate counterattack at Shiloh, near Memphis, Tennessee.

   a. Ulysses S. Grant
   b. George McClellan
   c. Robert E. Lee
   d. Stonewall Jackson

5. In 1862, the Union forces under McClellan were unable to capture the Confederate capital,

   a. Mobile, Alabama.
   b. New Orleans, Louisiana.
   c. Charleston, South Carolina.
   d. Richmond, Virginia.

6. In the Battle of _____, Lee invaded Maryland and the North for the first time.

   a. Second Manassas
   b. Antietam
   c. Fredericksburg
   d. Chancellorsville

7. After the battle of _____, Great Britain and France changed their minds about recognizing the Confederacy.

   a. Second Manassas
   b. Antietam
   c. Fredericksurg
   d. Chancellorsville

8. The Emancipation Proclamation of 1863

   a. declared escaped slaves contraband of war.
   b. freed slaves throughout the country.
   c. freed slaves in the Confederacy only.
   d. ignored slavery, but authorized black soldiers.

9. By May 1863, Robert E. Lee's Army of Northern Virginia

   a. had won most of its battles.
   b. had won at Fredericksburg, but lost at Chancellorsville.
   c. had been defeated by the Army of the Potomac at Fredericksburg.
   d. had been consistently defeated.

GETTYSBURG TO APPOMATTOX

Yet none of the Confederate victories was decisive. The federal government simply mustered new armies and tried again. Believing that the North's crushing defeat at Chancellorsville gave him his chance, Lee struck northward into Pennsylvania, in July 1863, almost reaching the state capital at Harrisburg. A strong Union force intercepted Lee's march at Gettysburg, where, in a titanic three-day battle—the largest of the Civil War—the Confederates made a valiant effort to break the Union lines. They failed, and Lee's veterans, after crippling losses, fell back to the Potomac.

More than three thousand Union soldiers and almost four thousand Confederates died at Gettysburg; wounded and missing totaled more than twenty thousand on each side. On November 19, 1863, Lincoln dedicated a new national cemetery at Gettysburg with perhaps the most famous address in U.S. history. He concluded his brief remarks with these words: " . . . we here highly resolve that these dead shall not have died in vain—that this nation, under God, shall have a new birth of freedom and that government of the people, by the people, for the people, shall not perish from the earth."

On the Mississippi, Union control was blocked at Vicksburg, where the Confederates had strongly fortified themselves on bluffs too high for naval attack. By early 1863, Grant began to move below and around Vicksburg, subjecting the position to a six-week siege. On July 4th, he captured the town, together with the strongest Confederate Army in the West. The river was now entirely in Union hands. The Confederacy was broken in two, and it became almost impossible to bring supplies from Texas and Arkansas.

The northern victories at Vicksburg and Gettysburg in July 1863 marked the turning point of the war, although the bloodshed continued unabated for more than a year and a half.

Lincoln brought Grant east and made him commander-in-chief of all Union forces. In May 1864, Grant advanced deep into Virginia and met Lee's Confederate Army in the three-day Battle of the Wilderness. Losses on both sides were heavy, but unlike other Union commanders, Grant refused to retreat. Instead, he attempted to outflank Lee, stretching the Confederate lines and pounding away with artillery and infantry attacks. "I propose to fight it out along this line if it takes all summer," the Union commander said at Spotsylvania, during five days of bloody trench warfare that largely characterized fighting on the eastern front for almost a year.

In the West, Union forces gained control of Tennessee in the fall of 1863 with victories at Chattanooga and nearby Lookout Mountain, opening the way for General William T. Sherman to invade Georgia. Sherman outmaneuvered several smaller Confederate armies, occupied the state capital of Atlanta, then marched to the Atlantic coast, systematically destroying railroads, factories, warehouses, and other facilities in his path. His men, cut off from their normal supply lines, ravaged the countryside for food. From the coast, Sherman marched northward, and by February 1865, he had taken Charleston, South Carolina, where the first shots of the Civil War had been fired. Sherman, more than any other Union general, understood that destroying the will and morale of the South was as important as defeating its armies.

Grant, meanwhile, lay siege to Petersburg, Virginia, for nine months, before Lee, in March 1865, abandoned both Petersburg and the Confederate capital of Richmond in an attempt to retreat south. But it was too late, and on April 9, 1865, surrounded by huge Union armies, Lee surrendered to Grant at Appomattox Courthouse. Although scattered fighting continued elsewhere for several months, the Civil War was over.

The terms of surrender at Appomattox were magnanimous, and on his return from his meeting with Lee, Grant quieted the noisy demonstrations of his soldiers by reminding them: "The rebels are our countrymen again." The war for southern independence had become the "lost cause," whose hero, Robert E. Lee, had won wide admiration through the brilliance of his leadership and his greatness in defeat.

1. In July 1863, after a victory at Chancellorsville, Robert E. Lee decided to invade

    a. Maryland.
    b. West Virginia.
    c. Pennsylvania.
    d. Tennessee.

2. The Confederate's advance was stopped at

    a. Fredericksburg.
    b. Gettysburg.
    c. Vicksburg.
    d. Pittsburgh.

3. Also in July 1863, Ulysses S. Grant captured _____, the last Confederate stronghold on the Mississippi.

    a. Fredericksburg
    b. Gettysburg
    c. Vicksburg
    d. Pittsburgh

4. Grant came east to take command and confront Lee at

    a. Chattanooga and Lookout Mountain.
    b. Atlanta and Charleston.
    c. the Battles of the Wilderness and Spotsylvania.
    d. Chancellorsville and Gettysburg.

5. Union forces gained control of Tennessee in 1864 with victories at

    a. Chattanooga and Lookout Mountain.
    b. Atlanta and Charleston.
    c. the Battles of the Wilderness and Spotsylvania.
    d. Chancellorsville and Gettysburg.

6. General Sherman left a broad swath of destruction while marching between

    a. Chattanooga and Lookout Mountain.
    b. Atlanta and Charleston.
    c. the Battles of the Wilderness and Spotsylvania.
    d. Chancellorsville and Gettysburg.

7. General Grant forced Lee to abandon _____ in March 1865.

    a. Chattanooga and Lookout Mountain.
    b. Atlanta and Charleston.
    c. the Battles of the Wilderness and Spotsylvania.
    d. Petersburg and Richmond.

132

8. Lee's attempt to retreat south ended on April 9, 1865, when surrounded, he surrendered at
   a. Charleston.
   b. Petersburg
   c. Richmond.
   d. Appomattox Courthouse.

PEACE DEMOCRATS, COPPERHEADS, AND DRAFT RIOTS

Throughout his presidency, Abraham Lincoln faced serious opposition to his political and wartime policies. Even in the North, the Civil War was so divisive and consumed so many lives and resources that it could hardly have been otherwise.

Opposition to Lincoln naturally coalesced in the Democratic Party, whose candidate, Stephen Douglas, had won forty-four percent of the free states' popular vote in the 1860 election.

The strength of the opposition generally rose and fell in proportion to the North's effectiveness on the battlefield. The first manifestation of dissatisfaction with the war effort—and by extension Lincoln—came not from the Democrats, however, but from the Congress, which formed the Joint Committee on the Conduct of the War in December 1861 to investigate the poor Union showing at Bull Run and Ball's Bluff. Dominated by radical Republicans, the Joint Committee pushed the Lincoln administration toward a more aggressive engagement of the war, as well as toward emancipation.

As might be expected from the party of "popular sovereignty," some Democrats believed that full-scale war to reinstate the Union was unjustified. This group came to be known as the Peace Democrats. Their more extreme elements were called "Copperheads."

Whether of the "war" or "peace" faction, few Democrats believed the emancipation of the slaves was worth shedding northern blood. Indeed, opposition to emancipation had long been party policy. In 1862, for example, virtually every Democrat in Congress voted against eliminating slavery in the District of Columbia and prohibiting it in the territories.

Much of the opposition to emancipation came from the working poor, particularly Irish and German Catholic immigrants, who feared a massive migration of newly freed blacks to the North. Spurred by such sentiments, race riots erupted in several northern cities in 1862.

With the Emancipation Proclamation of January 1863, Lincoln clearly added the abolition of slavery to his war aims. This was far from universally accepted in the North. In both Indiana and Illinois, for example, the state legislatures passed laws calling for peace with the Confederacy and retraction of the "wicked, inhuman and unholy" proclamation.

The North's difficulties in prosecuting the war led Lincoln, in September 1862, to suspend the writ of *habeas corpus* and impose martial law on those who interfered with recruitment or gave aid and comfort to the rebels. This breech of civil law, although constitutionally justified during times of crisis, gave the Democrats another opportunity to criticize Lincoln. Secretary of War Edwin Stanton enforced martial law vigorously, and many thousands—most of them southern sympathizers or Democrats—were arrested.

The Union's need for manpower led to the first compulsory draft in U.S. history. Enacted in 1863 to "encourage" enlistment, the draft further alienated many. Opposition was particularly strong among the Copperheads of Pennsylvania, Ohio, Indiana, and Wisconsin, where federal troops had to be called out to enforce compliance with it.

It must be noted that a man who was drafted could buy his way out for $300, about the equivalent of an unskilled laborer's annual income at that time. This feature added to the impression—strongly held in parts of the Confederacy as well—that this was a "rich man's war and a poor man's fight."

The most significant resistance to the draft took place in New York City in the summer of 1863. A Democratic Party stronghold, New York had already seen several draft officials killed that year. In July, a group of blacks were brought into the city, under police protection, to replace striking Irish longshoremen. At the same time, officials held a lottery drawing for the unpopular draft. The conjunction of the two events led to a four-day riot in which a number of black neighborhoods, draft offices, and Protestant churches were destroyed and at least one hundred and five people killed. It was not until several Union regiments arrived from Gettysburg that order could be restored.

The most celebrated civil case of the Civil War also took place that year. It concerned Clement Vallandigham, an aspiring Democratic candidate for the governorship of Ohio. Apparently seeking to bolster his candidacy, Vallandigham defied a local military ban against "treasonous activities" and attacked Lincoln's policies, calling for negotiations to end the war and terming it "a war for the freedom of the blacks and the enslavement of the whites." Union soldiers subsequently broke into his house and arrested him.

The legality of Vallandigham's arrest was immediately challenged by the Democrats and, indeed, some Republicans as well. Lincoln's response was to have him sent behind Confederate lines, where Vallandigham won the nomination. Making his way to Canada, he then carried out a boisterous, but unsuccessful, campaign.

Despite the Union victories at Vicksburg and Gettysburg in 1863, Democratic "peace" candidates continued to play on the nation's misfortunes and racial sensitivities. Indeed, the mood of the North was such that Lincoln was convinced he would lose his reelection bid in November 1864.

The Democratic candidate for president that year was General George McClellan, the man Lincoln had removed as commander of the Army of the Potomac two years earlier. McClellan's vice presidential candidate was a close ally of Vallandigham. Despite the hopes of the Democrats, however, McClellan refused to embrace the party's goal of negotiating an end to the war. Nonetheless, with victory at last within sight, Lincoln easily defeated McClellan in November, capturing every northern state except New Jersey and Delaware.

1. Opposition to the Civil War and emancipation was strongest among

    a. Radical Republicans.
    b. Peace Democrats and Copperheads.
    c. the Joint Committee on the Conduct of the War.
    d. Secretary of War Edwin Stanton.

2. In 1862,

    a. Democrats in Congress favored emancipation in the District of Columbia.
    b. Irish and German Catholics led race riots in the northern cities.
    c. the Emancipation Proclamation was promulgated.
    d. Indiana and Illinois legislatures called for peace and retraction of the Proclamation.

3. In 1863,

   a. Lincoln suspended *habeas corpus*.
   b. Lincoln imposed martial law.
   c. the first compulsory draft in U.S. history was passed.
   d. General George McClellan ran against Lincoln.

4. In July 1863, a combination race, draft, and religious riot occurred in

   a. Pennsylvania.
   b. Ohio.
   c. Wisconsin.
   d. New York City.

5. In 1864,

   a. Lincoln suspended *habeas corpus*.
   b. Lincoln imposed martial law.
   c. the first compulsory draft in U.S. history was passed.
   d. General George McClellan ran against Lincoln.

RECONSTRUCTION

For the North, the war produced a great hero in Abraham Lincoln—a man eager, above all else, to weld the Union together again, not by force and repression but by warmth and generosity. In 1864, he had been elected for a second term as president, defeating his Democratic opponent, George McClellan, the general whom Lincoln had dismissed after Antietam.

Lincoln's second inaugural address closed with these words:

> With malice toward none; with charity for all; with firmness in the right, as God gives us to see the right, let us strive on to finish the work we are in; to bind up the nation's wounds; to care for him who shall have borne the battle, and for his widow and his orphan . . . to do all which may achieve and cherish a just and lasting peace among ourselves and with all nations.

Three weeks later, two days after Lee's surrender, Lincoln delivered his last public address, in which he unfolded a generous reconstruction policy.

On April 14th, the president held what was to be his last Cabinet meeting. That evening, with his wife and a young couple who were his guests, he attended a performance at Ford's Theater. There, as he sat in the presidential box, he was assassinated by John Wilkes Booth, a Virginia actor embittered by the South's defeat. Booth was killed in a shootout some days later in a barn in the Virginia countryside. His accomplices were captured and later executed.

Lincoln died in a downstairs bedroom of a house across the street from Ford's on the morning of April 15th. Wrote poet James Russell:

> Never before that startled April morning did such multitudes of men shed tears for the death of one they had never seen, as if with him a friendly presence had been taken from their lives, leaving them colder and darker. Never was funeral panegyric so eloquent as the silent look of sympathy which strangers exchanged when they met that day. Their common manhood had lost a kinsman.

The first great task confronting the victorious North—now under the leadership of Lincoln's vice president, Andrew Johnson, a southerner who remained loyal to the Union—was to determine the status of the states that had seceded. Lincoln had already set the stage. In his view, the people of the southern states had never legally seceded; they had been misled by some disloyal citizens into a defiance of federal authority. And since the war was the act of individuals, the federal government would have to deal with these individuals and not with the states. Thus, in 1863, Lincoln proclaimed that if in any state ten percent of the voters of record in 1860 would form a government loyal to the U.S. Constitution and would acknowledge obedience to the laws of the Congress and the proclamations of the president, he would recognize the government so created as the state's legal government.

Congress rejected this plan and challenged Lincoln's right to deal with the matter without consultation. Some members of Congress advocated severe punishment for all the seceded states. Yet even before the war was wholly over, new governments had been set up in Virginia, Tennessee, Arkansas, and Louisiana.

To deal with one of its major concerns—the condition of former slaves—Congress, in March 1865, established the Freedmen's Bureau to act as guardian over African Americans and guide them toward self-support. And in December of that year, Congress ratified the 13th Amendment to the U.S. Constitution, which abolished slavery.

Throughout the summer of 1865, Johnson proceeded to carry out Lincoln's reconstruction program, with minor modifications. By presidential proclamation, he appointed a governor for each of the former Confederate states and freely restored political rights to large numbers of southern citizens through use of presidential pardons.

In due time conventions were held in each of the former Confederate states to repeal the ordinances of secession, repudiate the war debt, and draft new state constitutions. Eventually, a native Unionist became governor in each state with authority to convoke a convention of loyal voters. Johnson called upon each convention to invalidate the secession, abolish slavery, repudiate all debts that went to aid the Confederacy, and ratify the 13th Amendment. By the end of 1865, this process, with a few exceptions, was completed.

Both Lincoln and Johnson had foreseen that the Congress would have the right to deny southern legislators seats in the U.S. Senate or House of Representatives, under the clause of the Constitution that says, "Each house shall be the judge of the . . . qualifications of its own members." This came to pass when, under the leadership of Thaddeus Stevens, those congressmen (called "Radical Republicans") who sought to punish the South refused to seat its elected senators and representatives. Then, within the next few months, the Congress proceeded to work out a plan for the reconstruction of the South quite different from the one Lincoln had started and Johnson had continued.

Wide public support gradually developed for those members of Congress who believed that blacks should be given full citizenship. By July 1866, Congress had passed a civil rights bill and set up a new Freedmen's Bureau, both designed to prevent racial discrimination by southern legislatures. Following this, the Congress passed a 14th Amendment to the Constitution, which states that "All persons born or naturalized in the United States and subject to the jurisdiction thereof, are citizens of the United States and of the states in which they reside," thus repudiating the Dred Scott ruling which had denied slaves their right of citizenship.

All the southern state legislatures, with the exception of Tennessee, refused to ratify the amendment, some voting against it unanimously. In addition, in the aftermath of the war, southern state legislatures passed black codes, which aimed to reimpose bondage on the freedmen. The codes differed from state to state, but some provisions were common. Blacks were required to enter into annual labor contracts, with penalties imposed in case of violation; dependent children were subject to compulsory apprenticeship and corporal punishments by masters; and vagrants could be sold into private service if they could not pay severe fines.

In response, certain groups in the North advocated intervention to protect the rights of blacks in the South. In the Reconstruction Act of March 1867, Congress, ignoring the governments that had been established in the southern states, divided the South into five districts and placed them under military rule. Escape from permanent military government was open to those states that established civil governments, took an oath of allegiance, ratified the 14th Amendment, and adopted black suffrage.

The amendment was ratified in 1868. The 15th Amendment, passed by Congress the following year and ratified in 1870 by state legislatures, provided that "The rights of citizens of the United States to vote shall not be denied or abridged by the United States or any state on account of race, color or previous condition of servitude."

The Radical Republicans in Congress were infuriated by President Johnson's vetoes (even though they were overridden) of legislation protecting newly freed blacks and punishing former Confederate leaders by depriving them of the right to hold office. Congressional antipathy to Johnson was so great that for the first time in American history, impeachment proceedings were instituted to remove the president from office.

Johnson's main offense was his opposition to punitive congressional policies and the violent language he used in criticizing them. The most serious legal charge his enemies could level against him was that despite the Tenure of Office Act (which required Senate approval for the removal of any officeholder the Senate had previously confirmed), he had removed from his Cabinet the secretary of war, a staunch supporter of the Congress. When the impeachment trial was held in the Senate, it was proved that Johnson was technically within his rights in removing the Cabinet member. Even more important, it was pointed out that a dangerous precedent would be set if the Congress were to remove a president because he disagreed with the majority of its members. The attempted impeachment failed by a narrow margin, and Johnson continued in office until his term expired.

Under the Military Reconstruction Act, Congress, by June 1868, had readmitted Arkansas, North Carolina, South Carolina, Louisiana, Georgia, Alabama, and Florida to the Union. In many of these seven reconstructed states, the majority of the governors, representatives and senators were northern men—so-called "carpetbaggers"—who had gone south after the war to make their political fortunes, often in alliance with newly freed African Americans. In the legislatures of Louisiana and South Carolina, African Americans actually gained a majority of the seats. The last three Southern states—Mississippi, Texas, and Virginia—finally accepted congressional terms and were readmitted to the Union in 1870.

Many southern whites, their political and social dominance threatened, turned to illegal means to prevent blacks from gaining equality. Violence against blacks became more and more frequent. In 1870, increasing disorder led to the passage of an Enforcement Act severely punishing those who attempted to deprive the black freedmen of their civil rights.

As time passed, it became more and more obvious that the problems of the South were not being solved by harsh laws and continuing rancor against former Confederates. In May 1872, Congress passed a general Amnesty Act, restoring full political rights to all but about five hundred Confederate sympathizers.

Gradually, southern states began electing members of the Democratic Party into office, ousting so-called carpetbagger governments and intimidating blacks from voting or attempting to hold public office. By 1876, the Republicans remained in power in only three southern states. As part of the bargaining that resolved the disputed presidential elections that year in favor of Rutherford B. Hayes, the Republicans promised to end Radical Reconstruction, thereby leaving most of the South in the hands of the Democratic Party. In 1877, Hayes withdrew the remaining government troops, tacitly abandoning federal responsibility for enforcing blacks' civil rights.

The South was still a region devastated by war, burdened by debt caused by misgovernment, and demoralized by a decade of racial warfare. Unfortunately, the pendulum of national racial policy swung from one extreme to the other. Whereas formerly it had supported harsh penalties against southern white leaders, it now tolerated new and humiliating kinds of discrimination against blacks. The last quarter of the 19th century saw a profusion of "Jim Crow" laws in southern states that segregated public schools, forbade or limited black access to many public facilities, such as parks, restaurants, and hotels, and denied most blacks the right to vote by imposing poll taxes and arbitrary literacy tests.

In contrast with the moral clarity and high drama of the Civil War, historians have tended to judge Reconstruction harshly, as a murky period of political conflict, corruption, and regression. Slaves were granted their freedom, but not equality. The North completely failed to address the economic needs of the freedmen. Efforts such as the Freedmen's Bureau proved inadequate to the desperate needs of former slaves for institutions that could provide them with political and economic opportunity, or simply protect them from violence and intimidation. Indeed, federal army officers and agents of the Freedmen's Bureau were often racists themselves. Blacks were dependent on these northern whites to protect them from white southerners, who, united into organizations such as the Ku Klux Klan, intimidated blacks and prevented them from exercising their rights. Without economic resources of their own, many southern blacks were forced to become tenant farmers on land owned by their former masters, caught in a cycle of poverty that would continue well into the 20th century.

Reconstruction-era governments did make genuine gains in rebuilding southern states devastated by the war, and in expanding public services, notably in establishing tax-supported, free public schools for blacks and whites. However, recalcitrant southerners seized upon instances of corruption (hardly unique to the South in this era) and exploited them to bring down radical regimes. The failure of Reconstruction meant that the struggle of African Americans for equality and freedom was deferred until the 20th century—when it would become a national and not a southern issue.

1. Lincoln's Second Inaugural Address closed with the phrase

    a. "with malice towards none."
    b. "a nation divided against itself cannot stand."
    c. "we here highly resolve that these dead shall not have died in vain."
    d. "this nation, under God, shall have a new birth of freedom."

2. Lincoln was shot just five days after Lee's surrender, on

    a. April 14, 1864.
    b. April 14, 1865.
    c. April 15, 1864.
    d. April 15, 1865.

3. In December 1865, Congress

    a. advocated severe punishment for the Confederate states.
    b. created the Freedman's Bureau.
    c. ratified the 13th Amendment, which abolished slavery.
    d. elected Andrew Johnson president.

4. Andrew Johnson _____ Lincoln's generous reconstruction plans.

    a. repudiated
    b. abandoned
    c. modified
    d. carried out

5. Radical Republicans _____ Lincoln's generous reconstruction plans.

    a. significantly changed
    b. slightly altered
    c. carried out
    d. made no change to

6. The 15th Amendment

    a. made former slaves citizens.
    b. outlawed black codes.
    c. created five military districts.
    d. granted former slaves the right to vote.

7. Radical Republicans brought impeachment proceedings against Andrew Johnson because

    a. he so strongly opposed their punitive reconstruction plans.
    b. he was within his rights in dismissing the secretary of war.
    c. it was a dangerous precedent to remove a president over policy disagreements.
    d. the attempted impeachment failed by a narrow margin.

8. The elected officials of reconstructed states often were dominated at first by

    a. Confederate soldiers.
    b. loyal southern Unionists.
    c. military governors.
    d. carpetbaggers and newly freed African Americans.

9. The Democrats, who has opposed emancipation and the Civil War,

    a. held only three southern governorships by 1876.
    b. endorsed carpetbagger governments.
    c. protected the rights of blacks.
    d. negotiated for the end of Radical Reconstruction.

10. From the height of their power under Radical Reconstruction, by the end of the 19th century, African Americans in the South

   a. faced Jim Crow Laws and segregation.
   b. had the Ku Klux Klan to protect their rights.
   c. had southern Democrats to protect their rights.
   d. continued to prosper economically in the South.

Chapter 7
Questions for Further Research

1. Explain the economic, political, racial, and religious roots of Manifest Destiny and analyze how the concept influenced the westward expansion of the nation.

2. Explain the diplomatic and political developments that led to the resolution of conflicts with Britain and Russia in the period 1815–1850.

3. Compare President James K. Polk's resolution of the Oregon dispute with Great Britain and his initiation of war with Mexico.

4. Explain the causes of the Mexican-American War, the sequence of events leading to the outbreak of hostilities, and the provisions and consequences of the Treaty of Guadalupe Hidalgo.

5. Why did Mexico invite Americans to settle in Texas? Why did the conflict develop?

6. Describe the Texas rebellion and its aftermath.

7. Describe the annexation of Texas by the United States and the invasion of Mexico by U.S. troops, which led to war with Mexico.

8. Was the Mexican War justified? What might have happened if Mexican officials had agreed to negotiate with President Polk's ambassador? What else could Polk have done to prevent the war? What could the Mexican government have done?

10. What did the people known as "expansionists" believe and why? Did it contribute to the Mexican War? How did it lead to settlement of theOregon dispute with Great Britain and the acquisition of the Oregon territory?

11. Describe the Manifest Destiny and its appeal to 19th-century American industrial workers and small farmers.

12. What role did the annexation of Texas and the American desire for California play in leading to the outbreak of war between Mexico and the United States? Was the war justified? On what grounds did such critics as Abraham Lincoln, Frederick Douglass, and Henry David Thoreau oppose the war? On what grounds did supporters of President Polk's policies justify going to war? In what ways did the terms of the Treaty of Guadalupe Hidalgo reflect the spirit of Manifest Destiny?

13. Identify the issues surrounding the controversy over Oregon and evaluate Polk's campaign slogan "54 40' or fight." How practical was Polk's call for annexation of the entire Oregon Territory? Would it have been realistic for the United States to conduct a war over disputed territories with Mexico and Great Britain simultaneously? To what extent was the negotiated treaty of 1846 a satisfactory solution to interested parties in the United States and Great Britain?

14. How did the industrial revolution change the lives of Americans and create regional tensions?

15. How did the rapid expansion of slavery change the lives of Americans and create regional tensions?

16. How did the westward movement change the lives of American and create regional tensions?

17. How did the factory system and the transportation and market revolutions shape regional patterns of economic development, change the lives of men, women, and children?

18. Describe the rise of the labor and reform movements in the period before the Civil War.

19. Explain the major technological developments that revolutionized land and water transportation and analyze how they transformed the economy, affected international markets, and affected the environment.

20. Describe and evaluate national and state policies regarding a protective tariff, a national bank, and federally funded internal improvements.

21. Explain how economic policies related to expansion served different regional interests and contributed to growing political and sectional differences in the antebellum era.

22. Compare the effect of technological developments on business owners, farmers, and workers in different regions.

23. Identify and explain the factors that caused rapid urbanization and compare the new industrialized centers with the old commercial cities. How did rapid urbanization, immigration, and industrialization disrupt the social fabric of early 19th-century cities?

24. What accounted for increased emigration from Europe and for the growth of free black communities in the North?

25. To what extent were cities able to meet the demands and problems caused by rapid growth?

26. Explain how the cotton gin and the opening of new lands in the South and West led to the advance of "King Cotton" and to the increased demand for slaves.

27. Describe the plantation system and the roles of the owner and his family, of hired white workers, and of enslaved African Americans.

28. Identify the various ways in which African Americans resisted the conditions of their enslavement and analyzing the consequences of violent uprisings. Describe the Underground Railroad. Use personal accounts of the exploits of individuals escaping slavery.

29. Explain the lure of the West while comparing the illusions of migrants with the reality of the frontier.

30. Analyze cultural interactions among diverse groups in the trans-Mississippi region.

31. Describe the the origins and political organization of the Mormons, explaining the motives for their trek west and evaluating their contributions to the settlement of the West.

32. Describe and compare the overland trails west to Santa Fe, Oregon, Salt Lake, and California; the trail north from Mexico; and the water routes around the Horn and by way of Panama to California.

33. Describe the economic, social, and cultural differences between the North and the South.

34. Explain how events after the Compromise of 1850 contributed to increasing sectional polarization.

35. Describe the importance of the "free labor" ideology in the North and its appeal in preventing the further extension of slavery in the new territories.

36. How did the free labor system of the North differ from that of the South? To what extent did the different social and economic convictions contribute to tension between the North and the South?

37. Explain the causes of the Civil War and evaluate the importance of slavery as a principal cause of the conflict.

38. Describe the secession of the southern states, explaining the process and reasons for secession.

39. Explain how the military leaders and resources of the Union and the Confederacy affected the course and outcome of the Civil War. Compare population, armies, and leaders of the Confederacy with those of the Union at the beginning of the war.

40. Identify the innovations in military technology and explain their impact on humans, property, and the final outcome of the war.

41. How did political, military, and diplomatic leadership affected the outcome of the war?

41. Describe the provisions of the Emancipation Proclamation, Lincoln's reasons for issuing it, and its significance.

42. Describe the human costs of the war in the North and the South.

43. Contrast the Reconstruction policies advocated by Lincoln, Andrew Johnson, and sharply divided Congressional leaders, while assessing these policies as responses to changing events.

44. Describe the escalating conflict between President Johnson and Republican legislators, and explain the reasons for and consequences of Johnson's impeachment and trial.

45. Explain the provisions of the 14th and 15th Amendments and the political forces supporting and opposing each.

46. List the basic provisions of the 13th, 14th, and 15th Amendments. How were the lives of African American freedmen changed by these amendments? Did they obtain the rights and freedoms promised to them? How did the Ku Klux Klan attempt to block these rights?

47. What were the causes and consequences of the Compromise of 1877.

48. Explain the economic and social problems facing the South and appraising their impact on different groups of people.

49. Evaluate the goals and accomplishments of the Freedmen's Bureau.

50. How did African Americans attempted to improve their economic position during Reconstruction.

51. Was Reconstruction a revolution? What was the progress of "Black Reconstruction" and are legisative reform programs promoted by reconstructed state governments?

52. Why did corruption increase in the postwar period?

Made in the USA
Middletown, DE
02 July 2022

68312785R20082